PRAYER
AND PREACHING

Karl Barth

SCM PRESS LTD

BLOOMSBURY STREET LONDON

PUBLISHER'S NOTE

The first three chapters of this book have been compiled
from shorthand records made in the course of seminars held
by Professor Barth in Neuchâtel, Switzerland, 1947-49. The
records were transcribed by A. Perret and adapted by A.
Roulin. They were originally published as *La Prière* (Neuchâtel: Delachaux et Niestlé, 1953), and translated by Sara
F. Terrien for publication in USA as *Prayer* (Westminster
Press, 1952). The translation has been revised for this British
edition by B. E. Hooke.

The remaining chapters, also edited by A. Roulin, are explained by the author (pp. 64-6). They were published as
La Proclamation de l'Evangile (Delachaux et Niestlé, 1961),
and have been translated by B. E. Hooke. In the USA they
are published separately as *The Preaching of the Gospel*
(Westminster Press, 1963).

The editorial notes are supplied by the British publisher.

FIRST BRITISH EDITION 1964

© SCM PRESS LTD 1964

PRINTED IN GREAT BRITAIN BY
BILLING AND SONS LTD
GUILDFORD AND LONDON

PRAYER AND PREACHING

CONTENTS

PREFACE

by Professor James S. Stewart

It is an extraordinarily impressive fact that that greatest of theological giants St Paul, whose thoughts range through the universe, embracing in their width and scope and penetration the mysteries of life and death, things present and things to come, stands firmly based on 'the simplicity that is in Christ' (II Cor. 11.3). It is indeed this 'single-hearted devotion to Christ' (as the New English Bible translates it) that underlies both his profound insight into the divine wisdom and his revolutionary understanding of human existence.

Of Paul's greatest twentieth-century exponent, Karl Barth, the same could be said. His productivity has been immense, his horizons all-embracing, his domination of the contemporary theological scene unquestioned. Probably not since Calvin has there appeared a figure of like dimensions; and even those whose interpretation of the faith at many points is radically different have gladly confessed their indebtedness. Distinguished Roman Catholic theologians have listened attentively to this trumpet-toned Protestant voice, and have acknowledged the validity of this consuming quest of the truth. Yet the fact remains that this Colossus of a theologian is basically concerned with simple things; and no one reading Barth can have any doubt that the driving-force behind the mighty argument is the man's own single-hearted devotion to Christ. This is what makes the encounter with Barth, even through the printed page, a spiritual experience.

Ever since 1908, when he was ordained to the ministry of the Reformed Church, Barth has been a preacher. Only a theologian who was also a preacher could have written the epoch-making commentary on the Epistle to the Romans which in 1919 heralded a thoroughgoing revolution in biblical exegesis and exposition. Barth's own vivid description of what happened with that book was that it was just as if a man, climbing a church tower by night, should clutch at a rope to save himself from falling : the rope does indeed save him, but it is the bell rope, and the sudden pealing of the church bell through the darkness awakens the whole town.

Even in the monumental *Church Dogmatics* there are innumerable passages where the preacher in him takes command, and the argument catches fire in the passion of the evangelist. Just how searching and surgical this can be might be illustrated from a passage describing the resistance which the Word of God encounters even within the Church :

'The most cunning of all the stratagems which the resisting element in man can use in self-defence against the Word of grace is simply to immunize, to tame and harness. It is politely to take its seat in the pew, cheerfully to don the vestment and mount the pulpit, zealously to make Christian gestures and movements, soberly to produce theology, and in this way, consciously participating in the confession of Jesus Christ, radically to ensure that His prophetic work is halted, that it can do no more injury to itself, let alone to the world. May it not be that this most cunning of all defensive movements is also the most effective?'[1]

This little book on *Prayer and Preaching* demonstrates wonderfully Barth's characteristic union of simplicity and profundity. Certainly in these pages there is a Word from the Lord for the revitalizing of the Church.

New College,   JAMES S. STEWART
Edinburgh

---

[1] *Church Dogmatics,* IV 3, 1, p. 259.

I

PRAYER IN THE REFORMATION

BEFORE EMBARKING on the actual subject of prayer in the teaching of the catechisms produced by the Reformation, it may be useful to present some general observations suggested by these texts.

1. *The Reformers of the Church prayed.*

The Reformation appears to us as a great whole: a work of study, thinking, preaching, discussion, polemic, and organization. But it was more than all this. From what we know, it was also an act of continuous prayer, an invocation and, let us add, an action of certain men and, at the same time, a response on the part of God.

In Luther's Greater Catechism[1] there is a remarkable passage from which some sentences may be quoted:

> 'We know that our defence lies in prayer alone. We are too weak to resist the Devil and his servants. Let us hold fast to the weapons of the Christian; they enable us to fight the Devil. What has won these great victories over the undertakings of our enemies, which the Devil has used to enslave us, except the prayers of those good men who rose up like a rampart of brass to protect us? Our enemies may mock at us, but we shall defy them and the Devil if we continue steadfast in prayer. For we know that when a Christian prays thus: "Dear Father, thy will be done," God answers him, "Dear child, it shall be done in spite of the Devil and the whole world." '

There are some obscurities in the events of the sixteenth century, but here we touch upon a point of particular im-

[1] Martin Luther's *Catechisms* of 1529 are still standard summaries of faith among Lutherans.—Ed.

portance. Perhaps the faults and weaknesses which we observe at other moments of history are due to the fact that we no longer understand the meaning of these words of Luther's.

2. *The Reformers were of one mind concerning the importance and the significance of prayer.*

When the texts of the various catechisms are read and compared, it is possible to distinguish with some precision the dominant preoccupations peculiar to Luther, Calvin,[1] and the authors of the Heidelberg Catechism.[2] But it would be difficult, if not impossible to discover disagreement in the matter of faith. One of them, for example, emphasizes the fact that prayer is obedience to a command of God: man must pray because God wills it. One might suppose that this is Calvin, but in fact, it is Luther who holds this rigorous, almost military, idea: God commands, man must obey. Another insists that prayer is based on Christ's intercession with his heavenly Father. One might expect this to be Luther, but the words are Calvin's.

Calvin also insists that prayer must be addressed to God only, and not to saints or angels. Again we recognize the Genevan Reformer when he speaks of the part played by the Holy Spirit in prayer. On the other hand it is interesting to note that prayer is regarded, in the Heidelberg Catechism, as an act of thanksgiving.

We may also observe that the example and the reality of prayer are identical in all these texts. This ought to be understood in the discussions between Lutherans and Calvinists which still persist in Germany to this day. Since the Reformers were of one mind concerning prayer, they were in agreement on fundamentals; and if men can pray together they should also be able to take Communion

[1] John Calvin's *Catechism of the Church of Geneva* dates from 1545.—Ed.
[2] A document of 1562, modifying strict Calvinism in the interests of reconciliation with the Lutherans.—Ed.

together, for doctrinal differences can then be only secondary.

3. *One thing needs to be stressed: these texts do not make any distinction between individual and corporate prayer.*

For the authors of the catechisms the thing is quite simple: they see the Church, that is to say *us*, as members of a community forming a whole. But they also distinguish the individuals who constitute this whole. One cannot ask whether it is Christians who pray or the Church. There is no such alternative; for when Christians pray, it is the Church, and when the Church prays, it is Christians. There can be no opposition between these two.

Perhaps it is an indication of sickness in the Church that such questions as these can be asked: How ought I to pray, in my room, for my own spiritual needs? And how ought the Church, on its side, to pray? And so a special interest comes to be directed to prayer in the Church and the 'liturgical question'! Is this not a sign of disease?

For the Reformers there is no 'liturgical question': one prays in church *and* at home. They are not concerned to draw a distinction between private prayer and corporate prayer; what does concern them is the necessity of praying and praying well. This is perhaps a point which should be kept in mind. When secondary matters assume importance, it is the sign of some spiritual weakness.

4. *Another question is passed over in these texts: must one pray from the heart or according to a set form?*

Neither Luther nor Calvin paid heed to this question which exercises so many of our contemporaries. They insisted that it was necessary and right that a man's heart should pray; they stressed the sincerity of prayer as opposed to empty words. They knew what free prayer was, but they also knew that in real prayer the fancy cannot roam as it will: there must be discipline.

Jesus Christ not only told us to pray: in the 'Our Father' he also showed us how to pray, and we should do well to

keep to this rule. There must be feeling in prayer, as Calvin
says, but feeling must not be an excuse for the mind to
wander. The extempore prayers with which Calvin used to
end his sermons are remarkable for their stately uniformity;
he never indulged in unrestrained outpourings of words.
The same elements are always present: adoration of the
majesty of God and of the Holy Spirit, but they are not
stock phrases.

The Reformers were not fluent in prayer and it is doubtful whether they would willingly have spoken of a gift for
prayer. What they say is: Pray and pray well; this is what
matters. Be content to possess, in the 'Our Father', a model
for your prayers, but pray from the free impulse of the
heart.

5. *The Reformers do not distinguish between explicit
prayer (which is offered at specific times and expresses
itself outwardly by uttering certain words) and implicit
prayer (which finds expression, not in words but in feeling
and in a constant disposition of heart, conscience, and
mind).*

The 'pray without ceasing' of 1 Thess. 5.17 is not quoted
in any catechism of that period. It would seem that these
authors are chiefly concerned with explicit prayer, although
Calvin says that language is not always necessary. In
general it may be said that the teaching of the Reformers
as expressed in their writings, their preaching, and their
actions, shows that for them prayer is at once word,
thought, and life.

II

CHRISTIAN PRAYER
ACCORDING TO THE REFORMERS

W E SHALL consider the subject under three aspects: first, the problem of prayer; then prayer regarded as a gift of God; and, finally, prayer as an activity of man.

1. *The Problem of Prayer*

What place does prayer occupy in these catechisms? If you look through them you will notice that Luther deals first with the Commandments and then with the Creed, that is, the exposition of the faith. Calvin, however, begins with the Creed and the Commandments come afterwards. Thus he speaks of faith and then of obedience.

We Christians, therefore, regarded as believers and as obedient servants, are faced with a new problem, that of prayer. But is it really a new problem additional to faith and obedience? So it would seem. According to Calvin, prayer has to do with our life and our relation to the demands of this world. The question is, can I, as a Christian, really live according to the word of the Gospel and the Law, according to my faith and in obedience? Can I live thus amid the necessities of my existence? It is indeed possible to live in the holiness of obedience to the Gospel, as we are bidden to live and as we ought to live; but to do this we must listen to what we are told about prayer, we must ask God himself to come to our help, to teach us, to give us the power to walk in this path. This must be our quest, if we are to live, and the quest is prayer.

In Luther's catechism the situation of man at grips with faith and obedience is more closely examined. What is to be said, what can be done, in face of the fact that no one perfectly obeys the Law, while the Law demands perfect obedience, and whoever does not fulfil it perfectly does not fulfil it at all? However, we are believers, that is to say we have the beginnings of faith. Faith, in fact, is not something a man can possess as his own property. God says: 'Put your trust in me, believe in me.' And I go forward and believe; but even as I go forward I say: 'Help thou my unbelief.' Life is before us with its difficulties and its demands, and the Law is there also, requiring obedience in spite of our weakness and the obstacles which rise up before us. I go forward with only the meagre beginnings of faith; and I am commanded to advance, to become perfectly obedient, to pursue the path of faith on which I have taken but the first step.

On the one hand is our interior life, the life of weak and wilful men; on the other, our exterior life in this world with all its problems and difficulties. In addition there is the Divine Judgement which challenges us each moment saying: 'That is not enough.' And I may come to the point of asking myself: Are you, in truth, a Christian? In face of your meagre faith, your inadequate obedience, what do you mean when you say, 'I believe, I obey'? The gulf is immeasurably wide: we are challenged on all sides even when we believe and obey as well as we can. In such a situation (which is common to all Christians) prayer means turning to God, asking him to give us what we lack—power, strength, courage, serenity, prudence; to enable us to obey the Law and to keep his Commandments. And then, that he will grant us to go on believing and still believing and that he will renew our faith.

Such a request can be addressed only to God. As Calvin has said, this is a question of the honour we owe to his divinity, the honour due to him who has revealed himself to us by his Word. For it is the Word of God which upholds us in this situation in which prayer becomes a necessity.

Prayer means turning to him who has already spoken to us in the Gospel and the Law. It is he who confronts us when we are troubled by the imperfection of our obedience and the failure of our faith; he is the cause of our grief, and he alone can assuage it. We pray in order to ask him to do so.

Calvin points out that we are not alone in this difficult situation; we have Christian brothers and sisters from whom we may receive guidance and encouragement. But what men can do to relieve the wretchedness of our condition is simply to minister and dispense to us the good gifts of God : God himself does them the honour of using them to communicate his benefits to us and thereby puts us in their debt. Prayer therefore can in no way separate us from other men; rather, it unites us for it is something which concerns us all.

Before praying then, I first seek the company of other men. I know that you all experience the same difficulties as I do. Let us therefore take counsel together and give each other what we can. Nevertheless we cannot put our trust in our fellow creatures. There may be men able to speak to us of what we need or give us some indications of it, but the gift itself can only come from God. We cannot pray to men, not even to the saints.

In the sixteenth century it was necessary to assert that neither the saints of the Church nor the dead have power to help us. Perhaps, however, such a categorical statement might be questioned. I am not so sure that the saints of the Church cannot help us, for example, the Reformers and the saints who are alive on earth today. We live in communion with the Church of the past and receive support from it. But one thing is certain : neither living men nor those who are dead can be for us what God himself is to us : a present help in the great distress which is ours when faced by the

Gospel and the Law. The same thing is true of the angels, who can help us but may not be invoked.

Thus, for the Reformers, everything led back to this question : How am I to meet God? I have heard his word, I wish to listen to it in all sincerity, and here I am in my utter nothingness! The Reformers were not unaware that there are other difficulties besides this, but they knew that all are implied in this reality : I stand before God with my desires, my thoughts, my wretchedness; I must live with him, because to live means nothing else but to live with God. I am caught between the demands of life, both small and great, and the necessity of prayer. The Reformers tell us that the first thing is to pray.

2. *A Gift of God*

Prayer is a grace, a gift from God.

Like the Reformers, we shall not begin with an account of what a man does when he prays. Clearly he does something, he acts; but to understand that action we must begin at the end, that is to say, consider in the first place the answering of prayer. This may seem surprising for, logically, we should first ask what prayer is, and only afterwards, whether we are heard when we pray. But for the Reformers the vital point, the foundation of everything, is the certainty that God answers prayer. This is the first thing we must realize. Calvin says expressly that we obtain what we ask for. Prayer is grounded in that assurance.

Let us approach the subject by starting from the fact that God does answer; he is not deaf, he listens and, moreover, he acts. He does not act in the same way whether we pray or not. Prayer has an influence on the action, on the very existence, of God. That is the meaning of the word 'answering'.

In question 129 of the Heidelberg Catechism, it is stated that the answer to our prayers is more certain than our awareness of the things we ask for. It would seem that nothing can be more certain than our consciousness of what we are asking, but, according to this catechism, God's response is much more certain. We also must have this inward assurance. We may, perhaps, have doubts about the sincerity of our prayer and the worth of what we pray for; but the answer which God gives us is beyond all doubt. Our prayers may be feeble and inadequate, but what matters is not the strength of our prayers but the fact that God hears them; that is why we pray.

How does God answer us? Here we should recall the article on Jesus Christ in Calvin's catechism. There is no better way of understanding God's response than by keeping in mind this thought: Jesus Christ is our brother and we belong to him; he is the head of the body of which we are the members and, at the same time, he is the Son of God and himself God. He has been given to us as our mediator and our advocate before God. We are not separated from God and, more important, God is not separated from us. We may be godless, but God is not without men. This we must recognize and this is what matters. Confronting the godless is God who is never without men because in God man—all men and we ourselves—are present. God knows man, looks on him and judges him, but sees and judges him always in the person of Jesus Christ, his own Son, who was obedient and in whom he is well-pleased. Through him humanity exists in God. God looks on Christ and looks on us in him; we have one who represents us before God.

Calvin goes so far as to say that we pray through his mouth. Jesus Christ speaks by virtue of what he has been and what he has suffered in obedience and faithfulness to his Father; and we pray as it were through his mouth inasmuch as he enables us to draw near and be heard, and he intercedes for us. Thus, in truth, our prayer is already made even before we formulate it. When we pray we can only go back to that prayer which was uttered in the person of

Jesus Christ and is constantly repeated because God is not without man.

God is the Father of Jesus Christ, and that man, Jesus Christ, prayed and is praying still. Such is the ground of our prayer in Christ. This means that God has made himself surety for our requests, that he has himself willed to answer our prayers, because all our prayers are summed up in Jesus Christ; God cannot fail to answer because it is Christ who prays.

The fact that God yields to man's petitions, changing his intentions in response to man's prayer, is not a sign of weakness. He himself, in the glory of his majesty and power, has so willed it. He, who was man in Jesus Christ, by his own will is God and that is his glory and his almighty power. Therefore he suffers no diminishment in yielding to our prayer, but, on the contrary, by so doing he displays his greatness.

If God himself wills to enter into fellowship with man, to be as close to him as a father is to his child, this is no weakening of his power; God cannot be greater than he is in Jesus Christ. If God answers our prayers it is not simply because he hears us, or (as the efficacy of prayer is sometimes explained) in order to increase our faith, but because he is God—Father, Son, and Holy Spirit; God, whose Word was made flesh.

Let us now return to Luther, who calls us, or rather, orders us to pray. To abstain from prayer would be not to recognize that we stand before God, and hence to have a false idea of what God is. Such an attitude would render us incapable of grasping the fact that in Jesus Christ God meets us. When we become aware of this mystery, then we must pray; Jesus Christ, the Son of God, is there, and we who belong to him, who cannot do otherwise than follow him and speak through his lips, are with him. We have found the right road and now we have to walk on it. On this path the Gospel and the Law, the promise and the

Commandments of God, are one and the same. God opens this road to us and bids us pray. Thus it is not possible for us to say, I will pray, or I will not pray, as if it were a question of pleasing ourselves; to be a Christian and to pray mean the same thing, and not a thing which can be left to our own wayward impulses. It is, rather, a necessity, as breathing is necessary to life.

The Heidelberg Catechism makes it even more plain. It points out that prayer is quite simply the primary act of recognition towards God. The word 'recognition' is more precise than 'gratitude' because it means acting in accordance with what we recognize or know: everyone who knows God must express his recognition to him. He recognizes what God is and what he has done for man in Jesus Christ; he assumes the position which is ours in Christ, and in that position man must pray.

Luther even adds that God would be angry if we did not pray, for that would mean that we despised his gift to us. Since he himself bids us pray, how can we neglect to do so? Thus the Reformers remind us that we do not pray just when it suits us, but that prayer, in the life of a Christian, is an essential and necessary action in its own right.

Furthermore, God, because he is our God, of his grace causes us to pray; where the grace of God is, there men pray. God works in us, for we know not how to pray as we ought; it is the spirit of God that moves us and makes us capable of praying aright. We have no skill to judge whether we are worthy or able to pray or whether we have zeal enough to do so. Grace is itself the answer to such questions; when we are comforted by the grace of God, we begin to pray, with or without words.

God also shows us the way to set about praying. Prayer is not an arbitrary action nor yet something undertaken blindly. When we pray we cannot adventure according to our fancy in this or that direction, asking whatever we please, for God commands man to follow him and take the

place which he has assigned to him. This is regulated by
God, not by our initiative.

How ought we to pray? It is not by chance that Jesus
has given in the 'Our Father' a formula to teach men how
to pray aright. God himself shows us how we should pray,
for we have so many things to ask! And we think that what
we want is always so important! Besides it is necessary
that we should believe this. But so that our action may
become a real prayer, we must accept the offer that God
makes us. We cannot pray by ourselves, and if we suffer
disappointments in prayer, we must accept them as God's
means of showing us the way of true prayer. So he sets us,
with our needs and our problems, on a path by which we
may bring everything to him; but we must commit ourselves to that path. We need that discipline, and if it is
absent, we must not be surprised to find ourselves crying
out in a void instead of offering a prayer that is already
answered.

The Reformers bid us rejoice that we possess in the 'Our
Father' this pattern, by the use of which we may serve our
apprenticeship in true prayer. Calvin rightly declares that,
in the matter of prayer, we cannot act as aliens but, being
citizens of the city of God, we must accept its constitution,
its law, and its rules. Only on these conditions will there be
a response answering to the problems of our life.

Because he is our God in Jesus Christ, God himself
prompts us to assume before him an attitude that seems,
at first sight, to be rash and daring; he requires us to meet
him with a certain boldness. 'Thou hast made promises to
us, thou hast commanded us to pray; and now I come, not
with pious thoughts or because I like to pray (perhaps I
do not like praying) and I say to thee what thou hast told
me to say: help me in my necessity. Thou must do so, I
am here.' Luther is right: the position of a man who prays
demands not only utter humility but also a bold and manly
attitude. There is a good kind of humility, which consists in

freely accepting that place, in relation to God, which is ours in Jesus. If we are certain of what we are doing, and if we do not approach God on the strength of our own good intentions, then freedom is ours as a matter of course.

Thus God's good will towards us, that is, his mercy in Jesus, is a decisive factor in the matter which now concerns us. In question 117 of the Heidelberg Catechism it is stated that our firm foundation is the fact that God can hear our prayers, in spite of our unworthiness, owing to our Lord Jesus Christ.

3. *Prayer as Man's Action*

It follows from what has been said that prayer is quite simply the action by which we accept and make use of the Divine offer; an action in which we obey that commandment of the kingly grace which is the will of God. To be obedient to grace and to be thankful means that prayer is also an action on the part of man who knows himself to be a sinner and calls upon the grace of God. Man is confronted by the Gospel and the Law and by the feebleness of his own faith, even if he is not aware of it. We experience a certain sorrow and, at the same time, a certain joy; but we have not yet understood that we are sinners and that we do not achieve perfect obedience; we do not yet know that we are under a veil which must be removed. When we pray our human condition is laid bare to us and we are made aware of both our distress and our hope. It is God who places us in this situation, but at the same time he comes to our help. Prayer is therefore man's response when he understands his distress and knows that help is at hand.

We are not permitted to regard prayer as a good work to be performed, or a pious and pleasant duty. Prayer cannot be for us a means of achieving something, or making a gift to God and ourselves; we are in the position of a man who can only receive, who must now speak to God because there is no other to whom he can appeal. Luther said: We must all be destitute, for we are faced by a great emptiness and have everything to receive and learn from God.

Man's activity in prayer cannot be mere babbling, a stringing together of words or mutterings. The Reformers were emphatic on that point also. In the Roman Church there were many examples of the kind of prayer they were fighting against. This matter is equally plain and equally important for us today even if we are not Romans; prayer must be an act in which the feelings are engaged; it is not mere lip service, for God demands the allegiance of our hearts. If prayer is simply a formality, performed more or less correctly, if the heart has no part in it, it is nothing. Prayers made only with the lips are not merely superfluous, they are displeasing to God; not merely useless, but an offence against God. In this connexion, it is important to note, as Calvin points out, that prayer uttered in a language that neither the one who prays nor the congregation at prayer can understand, is a mockery of God, a perverse hypocrisy, for the heart cannot be in it. We must think and speak in a tongue that can be understood and that has a meaning for us.

Let us not pray just as we please, because then our un- ruly desires will have their way. Let us pray according to the rule given to us by one who knows our needs better than we ourselves do. He has directed us first to submit ourselves to him so that we may offer him our petitions. If we are to obey his order, we must, when praying, dismiss all such questions as: Does God hear us? On this point Calvin states categorically 'Such prayer is not prayer.' There is no possible excuse for doubting, for it goes with- out saying that we shall be heard. Even before praying we must assume that we have been heard.

We are not free to pray or not to pray, nor to pray only when we feel so inclined, for prayer is not an activity which is natural to us. Prayer is a grace, and we can expect this grace only from the Holy Spirit. This grace is with God and his Word in Jesus Christ. If we accept this, and if we receive what God gives, then all is done, everything is in order, not as the result of our good pleasure but in the freedom to obey him which is ours.

Above all, let us not suppose that man is entirely passive, that he can relax in an arm-chair as it were, and say : 'The Holy Spirit will pray for me.' By no means. Man is impelled to pray, he must do so. Prayer is an action as well as a supplication to the Lord that he will put us in that posture which is pleasing to him. This is one aspect of the problem of grace and freedom : one labours, but all the time one knows very well that it is God who wills to make our work effective. Our human freedom is not destroyed by God's freedom; one submits oneself to the action of the Holy Spirit, but nevertheless one's own mind and heart are not asleep meanwhile. Such is prayer considered as a human activity.

By being loyal to the work of God we can share in that work. It is a great thing to preach, to believe, to obey— even in our imperfect way—the Commandments of God. But in every expression of faith and obedience, it is prayer that brings us into a relationship with God and allows us to be fellow-workers with him. God calls us to live with him and our answer is : 'Father, I desire to live with thee.' Then he says to us : 'Pray, call on me; I hear you, I will live and reign with you.'

The Reformation was not carried out without the work of Luther, Calvin, and many others. God was working by causing them to share in his work. It was not through the brilliance of their virtue, their wisdom or their piety that God was able to accomplish his work with them, but through their humility and their boldness in prayer. And God calls us, as single individuals and in community, to take part in such prayer, which is an act both of humility and of victory. This act is demanded of us because we are given the power to perform it.

III

THE INTERPRETATION OF THE LORD'S PRAYER ACCORDING TO THE REFORMERS[1]

1. *Our Father in Heaven*

WE ARE bidden to pray. This presupposes everything that has been said above about prayer in general. But this is the important point: we are told to pray: *Our Father who art in heaven.* It is Jesus Christ who bids us call on God and address him as our Father; Jesus Christ who is the Son of God, who has made himself our brother and makes us his brothers. He takes us with him, to make us his companions, and places us at his side, so that we may live and act as his brothers and members of his body. He says to us, 'Follow me.'

The 'Our Father' is not just any form of prayer to be used by anyone, no matter who; it presupposes 'us': Our Father; one who is a Father to us in a unique way. This 'us' derives from Jesus Christ's command to follow him; it implies that the man who prays is in communion with Jesus Christ and dwells in the brotherhood of the sons of God. Jesus Christ calls, allows, commands man to be joined with him, more especially in his intercession with God, his Father. Jesus Christ calls us, commands us, allows us to speak with him to God, to pray his prayer with him, to be

[1] At the beginning of his exposition Professor Barth warned his hearers that he did not propose to confine himself to a historical summary of the Reformers' teaching on the Lord's Prayer, but that, having carefully studied the writings of Luther and Calvin and thoroughly assimilated their thought, he would allow himself to treat the texts with a certain freedom.—Ed.

united with him in the Lord's Prayer, and thus to adore God, to pray to God and to praise him with one voice and one soul in union with Christ himself.

This 'us', moreover, means that the man who prays is in communion with all those who are in his company and who, like him, are bidden to pray; who have received the same call, the same command, the same permission to pray at Christ's side. We pray 'Our Father' in the fellowship of that company, that congregation which we call the Church (the *ecclesia*).

But while we are in communion with the saints, the *ecclesia* of those who are gathered together by Jesus Christ, we are also in communion with those who, perhaps, do not pray as yet but for whom Christ prays, since he prays for all mankind. Mankind is the object of his intercession and we, therefore, enter into this communion with all mankind. When Christians pray, they are, so to speak, substitutes for all those who do not pray; and, in this sense, they are in communion with them, in the same way as Jesus Christ has made himself one with sinful man and lost humanity.

Our Father: thou who hast begotten us, brought us into being by thy Word and thy Spirit; thou who art our Father because thou hast created us, the Lord of the Covenant which thou hast been pleased to make with man, thou in whom and with whom our life began, and in whom it finds its completion.

Our Father: on whom our whole existence in time and eternity depends; God the Father, whose glory is our inheritance, whom we may freely approach, like children to their father!

Our Father, thou who by nature art always ready to hear us and to answer us. But we constantly forget it. . . . We may deny God, but he can never forget us or deny us. The Father, by his very nature, is faithful; he is high above us for ever and his good will towards us can never change.

That is what God is to us. But we must admit that we

have no right to address him thus, to be his children or to approach him in this way. He is our Father and we are his children in virtue of the natural relationship which exists between him and Jesus Christ, in virtue of that fatherhood and that sonship which actually existed in the person of Jesus Christ, and which have reality for us in him. We are his children and he is our Father in virtue of that new birth accomplished at Christmas, on Good Friday and at Easter, and made effective at our baptism. A new birth, that is to say, a completely new order of being, a life entirely different from what our human potentialities or merits could produce.

God our Father means our merciful Father; we ourselves are and always will be prodigal sons who can claim no rights save the one given to us in the person of Jesus Christ.

This does not imply any diminution of what has been said about the divine fatherhood. The splendour and the certainty, the very greatness and majesty of our Father are manifested in the fact that we stand before him without power or worth, without real faith and with empty hands. And yet, in Christ, we are God's children. We can contribute nothing whatever of our own to make the reality of that sonship more certain : divine reality alone is the fulness of all reality.

Jesus Christ is the source and the warrant for the divine Fatherhood and our sonship; for this reason that fatherhood and that sonship are incomparably superior to all the relationships among ourselves which we denote by the terms father, son, children. These human relationships are not the original of which the other could be the image or symbol. The true and original fatherhood and sonship subsist in the bonds which God has created between himself and us. Anything that exists among us is only the image of that original sonship. When we call God our Father, we are not using symbols, but are experiencing the full reality of the words 'father' and 'son'.

Who art in heaven. Heaven is part of the created world; that part of creation which is on high, unapproachable, incomprehensible. This means that God, who is high above and beyond the heavens, is also the Father of Jesus Christ, in whom he loves the world. If God is described as boundless, incomprehensible, free, sovereign, eternal, omnipotent, transcendent, the true meaning of these words does not derive from any idea or abstraction intended to define the opposite of what is limited, comprehensible and temporal. All these attributes derive their real meaning from the goodness of the heavenly Father who has made himself our Father in Jesus Christ. Here lies the meaning of his transcendence, his existence beyond the heavens. No philosophy, whether that of Aristotle, Kant, or Plato, can apprehend the transcendence of God, for philosophers can only reach the edge of that incomprehensible which is far higher than ourselves. All philosophy finds its turning point in the heavens; but the Gospel speaks to us of him who is in heaven and beyond the heavens. No spiritualist, idealist or existentialist can lead us to the reality of God in his transcendence, which is not the same as spirit or invisibility. God's transcendence is displayed, revealed, and actualised in Jesus Christ, the depth of his omnipotent mercy.

God exists supremely in heaven, which is his throne; there he confronts our desires, our needs, great and small, our ideals, our principles, our wisdom and our stupidity, our humanism and our brutishness. There is the judge, the king whose subjects we are, who reigns, at times in opposition to us, but nevertheless over us always. He is ever the same and yet never the same for he is new every morning; he is present to us at every moment, and he is eternal only by being present to us. He is free grace and gracious freedom, the one to whom all things are subject and all is entrusted; in whose hands everything can and must be of use, has been and will be used. This is the one to whom we speak, not on our own initiative but because we are bidden

and called to do so. We are at liberty to approach him,
but this liberty is his gift, it does not belong to us by
nature. It is the liberty of the children of God, the liberty
of the Word and the Spirit.

2. *The Petitions*

Let us begin by considering the petitions as a whole. We
note that the arrangement of these petitions is, in a sense,
analogous to that of the ten Commandments: there is a
very distinct difference between the first three and the last
three; the former correspond to the first four Commandments and the latter to Commandments five to ten. The first
three petitions are concerned with the glory of God; this
is where the 'Our Father' begins. Thus we are permitted, or
rather commanded, to commit ourselves to God's cause, to
pray that this cause—God's name, his kingdom, his will—
may triumph and so reach its fulfilment. God has revealed
himself in Jesus Christ as one who, while enjoying perfect
freedom and self-sufficiency, yet does not will to be alone.
He does not desire to act, exist, live, labour, work, strive
and conquer, reign and triumph apart from man. Therefore
it is not his will that his cause should be his alone; he
desires it to be man's cause also.

Can there really be atheists, men without God? At all
events, even if there are men without God, there cannot be,
in Christian terms, God without men. It is very important
to realize this: God has been with us, he is with us,
Emmanuel! He permits us, he commands us to pray, as in
these first three petitions we are bidden to do, for the
triumph of his cause. He invites us to take part in his work,
in his government of the Church and of the world. When
we pray, '*May thy Name . . . thy Kingdom . . . thy
Will . . .*', we put ourselves on God's side, no less. God
invites us to unite ourselves with his purposes and his
actions, and it should be noted that this invitation comes
at the beginning and is repeated at the end, in the doxology.

On these three petitions depend the liberty, the joy, the eagerness and the assurance of the other supplications. All our entreaties presuppose that we desire to take our part in the cause of God. Anyone who refused to do so, who had no concern for God's cause, would not know how to pray for the forgiveness of his sins or for his daily bread; he would not understand what it meant. We cannot live with God unless we are in agreement with his purposes, with his cause, which includes ours and all others. Otherwise we might as well try to stand in mid air. We must have ground to walk on, and in prayer we walk on the ground of these first three petitions. It is not surprising that so many prayers echo in a void and are not heard or answered. And yet everything would be quite simple if it were understood that one must begin at the beginning; there is no other way of praying.

The last three petitions concern us directly and vitally; they relate to our comfort, our good will, and our salvation, bodily as well as spiritual and heavenly. Because God, in Jesus Christ, has united our cause (the important and the trifling problems of our life) to his own, we are permitted, we are indeed commanded, to appeal now quite simply on our own behalf. And here our whole life is at stake. We are not merely given leave, but we are ordered to bring to God and entrust to him all our baggage (for we do not journey through this world without amassing a very complicated collection of baggage). We can entrust to God all this impedimenta—temporal, material and secular as well as eternal, Christian, ecclesiastical and theological.

In Jesus Christ the human being is revealed; in him humanity becomes pre-eminently a creature which cannot exist or act by itself; it cannot live without God; it can neither eat nor drink, love nor hate; it cannot justify or save itself, sorrow or rejoice, hope or despair, experience, success or failure. It is thanks to God that we exist among his creatures. Thus, in fact, there are no men without God.

There are people who believe themselves to be atheists, and cling firmly to that idea. But this makes no difference whatever; man as such does not exist apart from God; he may behave like a naughty child that screams and scolds its mother—but the mother is still there.

This is not a philosophical concept. It is doubtful whether the statement, 'man does not exist without God' could be convincingly explained apart from faith in Jesus Christ. But once we have understood what Jesus Christ is, we understand what man is and how he cannot be separated from God. Because, therefore, there cannot be man without God (for atheism is an absurd invention), God commands us to pray; God shares in all our concerns, in our needs, our cares, our sorrows and our expectations. When we pray, *Give us our bread*, we plainly declare what our life really is; we admit, what is indeed the truth, that without him we are nothing. And this command, this invitation to pray to him, to make our cause one with his, is a plain declaration of what is: God bids us and commands us to place ourselves at the side of Jesus Christ who deigned to assume humanity. He was God and he became man. Thus he concerns himself with everything, great and small—and especially the small things—with which we are concerned.

Man's cause—his material needs and his salvation— comes after God's. But it should be noted that there is no question here of optional requests. The first three petitions would certainly not exist were it not for the last three, which are as indispensable as the others. The man who did not go on praying the last three petitions would not be praying sincerely, for he too must have his place, since his own cause is involved, all he is, with his temperament, his nerves and the rest. He is not there on account of God's cause only; he needs must bring his own also and make it enter into God's. It would be dangerous, therefore, to omit the last three petitions, for then there would be, on the one hand, an ecclesiastical, theological and metaphysical sphere and, on the other, a sphere concerned with money, sex, business and social relations. There would be two compartments. But, whether we like it or not, there is only one compartment and nothing is more fatal than the illusory notion of two compartments. You know how often ministers imagine that there are these two: this contrast between God's cause and ours. But in fact they are bound together, and we pray for both at once. This is so because it is Jesus Christ who bids us pray with him and in him these two causes are one. It is important, therefore, to understand not only the difference between the two parts of the Lord's prayer, but also their unity.

Let us recall that Luther, in his Shorter Catechism, lays stress, in an interesting and enlightening manner, on this paradox: that God's actions take the same course as our prayer; he sanctifies his name, his kingdom comes, his will is done, he gives us our bread, he forgives us; and he does all this before we ask it. We speak to him who has heard us before we have said anything to him. Let us not forget this—and Luther was right to say so—it is Jesus Christ who prays and we join in his intercession. It is he whom God hears, and his prayer has been heard since the beginning of the world from eternity to eternity; all is already in order. In the first part of this book I stressed, as Luther and Calvin did, the fundamental facts of prayer and response. Let us begin by understanding this: we are heard in the name of Jesus Christ. Everything is already there when we approach God.

Luther says, concerning the Lord's Prayer, that we must take our part in God's activity. God is working for his glory and our salvation, and we should profit by his action, not as spectators nor yet by assuming the part of indispensable fellow-workers, but by praying and by concerning ourselves with him and with what he is doing. This is real collaboration. He bids us approach him in the knowledge that his cause and ours are one, for our cause is embraced by his.

We men come to him, therefore, and stand before him, prepared to live in the total concord of these two causes. All is contained within the liberty and the sovereignty of God. This is not necessity or fate, but God is our Father and he wills that we should be with him.

3. *Hallowed Be Thy Name*

When we speak of God's 'name', we mean that which represents the glory of God in the created world. Not simply and directly to be identified with God himself, the name is the representation of God. Because the created world is the theatre where the glory of God is displayed (Calvin), the world is a creature merely; in certain conditions (which do not depend on itself), it can become the bearer of God's name (though not in any strict philosophical sense). There may be in the world signs, as it were, of God's name, indications of the presence of God himself, and if so, it might be said that these signs are not invisible but are illuminated like the advertisements in our cities, illuminated by Revelation.

Our eyes are opened for us to see them; the world is God's world, and therefore his name can be written on it; the universe can sing his praise; everything that God has created can bear the name of its Creator.

And now let us ask ourselves; *Is* that name visible? *Is* it revealed? *Are* these signs illuminated? *Are* our eyes and ears opened? *Is* his name hallowed? We realize that such a consummation is not within the power of any created thing; creation cannot, of itself, become the bearer of the Divine name. The world as such has no power to reveal God; neither is man, as such, capable of receiving a revelation whether through sight, hearing or understanding. It is God who speaks aright of God (Pascal). God by his own action—at once objective and subjective—causes himself to be seen, and is seen, known, and truly recognized, and he enables us to live in this world in his presence, knowing and recognizing him. This Divine action becomes real for us in prayer.

The prayer 'Hallowed be thy name' implies that the name of God is known to him who prays, for no one prays for something which he does not know. This presupposes that the name of God is already hallowed (as Luther said). Thus, in this special situation of those who pray the 'Our Father' with Jesus Christ, we also attempt in prayer, to obey his command to follow him. And as we pray with Jesus Christ we are not unaware of the hallowing of God's name in the past as well as in the present.

This prayer is, then, a response before we formulate it. We would not be Christians praying with Jesus Christ if our prayer meant that we knew nothing of that hallowing. In fact we are praying that what is happening already through God's action may continue and reach its fulfilment. The words *Hallowed be thy name* should therefore be written in this way: 'this name is already hallowed', for this presupposition is the basis of prayer.

Our Father in heaven, thou hast spoken to us. In thy Son, who is thy Word, thou hast made thyself palpable and accessible to us in the flesh, in this world. The signs of thy name are luminous; we are not alone in this world, for thou dost show thyself to us in a human form so that we can understand what thou sayest to us. We do not live in a world without God. Thy prophets and apostles speak to us on the level of our own life and we hear them. Thy Church, the assembly of those whom thou hast called and still dost gather together, lives on earth and has survived through many centuries, in the midst of countless upheavals, in fear and weakness; and, in spite of all that can be said about its faults, we have heard thy voice through thy Church and its work.

We are baptized, we have our being in that Church, among thy children, being ourselves thy children, and among thy missionaries whom thou hast charged to pro-claim thy word, and one cannot be a child of God without

B

being a missionary. We are free to believe, to will, to obey.
This means that the world—this world in which we live—
and our own lives with their limitations, their burdens,
their difficulties, their problems and those of our neighbours
—all this can no longer be for us an insoluble mystery.
There are mysteries in plenty but we do not live in a
mystery of utter darkness, we are not surrounded by
nothingness. The doctrine of Sartre and Heidegger, which
would plunge us again into paganism, is not true. We know
that in this world and in human history one thing is certain : the signs of thy presence are shining lights : Jesus
Christ died and rose again for us, and not for us only but
for the whole world. Thus man's hope lies in this fact that
God loved the world. Such is the reality made manifest in
the death and resurrection of the Lord. And we live in the
recollection of that fact and in the expectation of the
general resurrection. This is the sense in which we say that
God's name is already hallowed; this is the Christian position. The key to the mystery is in our hands.

To continue : because this key is given to us, because the
name of God is already hallowed, we have all the more
reason to pray : 'Hallowed be thy name.' That is to say,
*that it may be granted to us and to the world—this world
which is neither better nor worse than we are, and in
which we thy creatures have the privilege of knowing thee
and being called to thy service—that it may be granted to
us to profit by thine incomparable gift; that the word thou
hast spoken through thy Son may not have been spoken in
vain; that thy Church may know how to make the most of
its life, that it may be delivered from all Romanizing
reaction and all impatient Americanism, from fear and
cowardice, from pride and cant; that we may give up dip-
ping into the Bible instead of reading it; that there may be
less quoting from the Bible and more living with it and
letting it speak to us. We pray that the Bible will not cease
to be important to us, that it may never bore us, that no*

part of thy word shall become, in our minds or on our lips, a tedious matter, a poor sermon, bad teaching or bad theology. This is all very simple but also very necessary.

Luther has explained at some length that this hallowing must manifest itself in preaching; a bad sermon has just the opposite effect. May the Word of God become for us each day anew the Word of God; may it be not a truth, a principle, something laid upon a table, but a living person, something of the greatest mystery and the greatest simplicity! And may the signs of God's name and God's word be made visible through us and among us by the austerity and the serenity of our lives, our behaviour, and our habits. We pray that it may be granted to us to display in our lives that great joy and peace which we so often talk about, so that others may notice them. We pray that the pride and ignorance and unbelief by which Christians continually dishonour God may be checked and suppressed, if only a little.

May this key which has been placed in our hands be turned even a little, so that one day the door can be opened! This is the hallowing of God's name. We can see that there is reason to pray for these good things and this consummation, so that what still remains to be done and what we ourselves cannot do, shall come to pass. But in order that all this may be brought about, God himself must intervene, for his cause is at stake. We who are responsible are so ill-qualified to uphold this cause. How overwhelming is our responsibility in this undertaking; and how absolutely necessary it is for God himself to intervene lest we should be found among those foolish virgins who had no oil!

4. *Thy Kingdom Come*

We have to go somewhat farther than the Reformers, who failed, here as elsewhere, to perceive the eschatological character of that reality which is the Kingdom of God.[1] We

---

[1] I.e., that the Kingdom comes with the end of the world as we know it.—Ed.

shall, therefore, give a slightly amended version of their teaching.

The Kingdom of God, in the New Testament, is the life and purpose of the world in accordance with the intentions of the Creator; it is the effective and appointed defence against the inevitable consequence of sin, against the mortal danger, the annihilation which lay in wait for the world because it is merely a creature. The Kingdom of God is the final victory over sin; it is the reconciliation of the world with God (II Cor. 5.19). And the consequence of that reconciliation is a new world, a new age, a new heaven and a new earth, which are new because they have entered into and are enfolded by the peace of God.

The Kingdom of God is the righteousness of God, the Creator and the Lord who justifies and triumphs. The destiny and purpose of the world is the coming of the Kingdom: 'thy Kingdom come'. Clearly we are once more confronted with a consummation which infinitely exceeds our powers, since all we are and all we can do, even in the most favourable conditions, is threatened by the same danger. We ourselves are in need of that deliverance, that victory, that reconciliation, that renewal. The coming of the Kingdom is in no sense dependent on our power; we are no more able to assist its coming than is creation itself, which is the image of what we are and can do. But it is for us an object of prayer. God alone, who created the world, can bring about its completion in that act of fulfilment in which he vindicates himself and his cross. The Kingdom means the peace and righteousness of the world brought to perfection, and this can only come to pass by the work of God. We must therefore pray that his Kingdom may come and that he may cause the bell to sound the hour of crisis.

But saying to God 'Thy Kingdom come' presupposes that he who prays thus has some knowledge of that Kingdom, that life, that righteousness, that newness, that reconciliation; that these things are not without meaning for him.

He must know also that wherever this prayer is offered the Kingdom has already come.

Once again we are in the amazing position of those who pray 'Our Father' in the fellowship of Jesus Christ and those who are his. *Thy Kingdom come* is equivalent to : 'Thy Kingdom is already come; thou hast established it in our midst.' 'The Kingdom of God is among you' (Luke 17.21). *Thou, God the Father, hast accomplished all things in Jesus Christ; in him thou hast reconciled the world to thyself!*

St Paul does not speak of this reconciliation as a future event. He says 'He *has* reconciled'; it is done. *In Jesus Christ thou hast abolished sin and all its consequences; thou hast destroyed all alien and hostile powers.* 'I saw Satan like lightning fall from heaven' (Luke 10.18). *Thou hast removed the mortal peril which threatened our lives. Thou, O God, in Jesus Christ didst become the new man who will never die. It is done. In him thy Kingdom has appeared in this world, in all the depth and height of its glory, undiminished and unconcealed.*

In Jesus Christ the world has reached its end and its goal. Thus, the last judgment and the resurrection of the dead have already been wrought in him; this is not only an event to be awaited, it is already behind us. When the Church speaks of Jesus Christ, when she proclaims his word, when she believes the Gospel and makes it known to the heathen, and when she prays to God, she looks back to her Lord who is already come. She calls to mind Christmas, Good Friday, Easter and Pentecost. These are not just some historical events to which we may attach a religious significance (with the private conviction that in itself this is of no importance). On the contrary, this is everything that has ever happened and is behind us. We proclaim the Word made flesh and the Kingdom of God which has come. The Church is not and cannot be insistent if she does not rejoice, if she is in doubt. A sorrowful and gloomy Church is not the Church! For the Church is built on him who was made flesh, who came to say the last word (not the last but one). This last word has already been uttered and on it our life depends; nothing in it can be changed. The age which began with Christmas and Easter cannot be reversed.

What does this mean when we truly understand it and live by it? It means that we have all the more reason to pray: *Thy Kingdom come!* There is no contradiction here, and one for whom these things are true is well aware of it; that is why he prays.

It means also that God's great initiative on behalf of man, which began at Christmas and Easter and Pentecost, must be resumed so that it may not be simply something that is past and behind us; for we do not live by looking backwards only, but by looking forward also. It must come, the future must bear the stamp of the past, our past must become our future, and the Lord who has come must come again.

We pray for the removal of the covering which now conceals all things, as a cloth covers a table; the table is underneath though you cannot see it, but the cloth has only to be removed for the table to be seen. We pray that the covering which still veils the reality of the Kingdom may be removed, so that the reality of all those things which have already been changed in Jesus Christ may be seen. Here is the profoundest depth of God's truth, which immeasurably surpasses all else. Our private lives and the lives of our families, the life of the Churches, political events—these are the veil behind which lies reality. As yet we do not see face to face, but only dim reflections as in a mirror. We cannot be sure where we stand when we read the papers, not even the religious papers. So that we may see what truly is, 'thy Kingdom' must come, Jesus Christ must become visible, as he was at Easter, as he showed himself to his apostles. He will be, he is even now, head of the new mankind of the new world. We know this, but as yet we do not see it; we are waiting to see it; we walk by faith, not yet by sight.

May the radiance of God, manifested in Jesus Christ, in his life, his death, and his resurrection, shine upon us, on our whole life and on all things! May the secret of earthly life be revealed, that secret which has already been revealed though as yet we do not see it—hence the anxiety, the cares, the false ideas and the despairs in which we live! We do not understand, and we pray that it may be granted to us to see and understand.

To return now to the interpretation of the Reformers. When we pray, may it be granted to us also to see, even now, at least the first signs of that new age and of that victory which is already won; may the dawn of the universal day enable us to see ourselves and others, and the incidents of our history, in the light of that which is to come. This total revelation, this *apokalypsis* (I Pet. 1.13), will be given to us. May our faith in him who has come be made alive! This can only come to pass if faith is founded on what has happened in the past and looks towards what is to come, which will reveal the universality of what he has accomplished. May it be granted to us to live in that hope. It is not possible to say: 'Thy Kingdom come!' if we are without hope for our own time, for today and tomorrow. The great Future with a capital F is also a future with a small f. This is enough to make us realize, at least in part, how totally inadequate is everything we do in this present time; it brings home to us the triviality of so many of the conflicts in which we are engaged, especially our private, psychological conflicts which, ultimately, are quite unnecessary. But to understand this, we must be able to see the Kingdom which is to come; psychologists cannot help us. One day the sun will rise and full knowledge will be ours. We have only to wait till Easter becomes actual for all the world; then we shall have no more need of psychologists because there will be perfect health. It is astonishing

to note how we Swiss—even more ingenuously than other
modern Europeans—occupy ourselves with psychology,
whereas in Germany, for example, all such conflicts have
disappeared under the pressure of life and its demands.
When there is life, there are no more psychological problems.

We pray that it may be granted to us to see the futility
of this tragic sense, which befits pagans but not Christians;
that we may live in serenity, with good will, and in charity
which constrains no one but has the power to attract everyone in some measure.

A variant reading in the Lucan text of the Lord's Prayer
(Codex Bezae) adds the words: 'That thy Holy Spirit may
come upon us and purify us.' Even though only the accepted
texts of Matthew and Luke are authentic, this variant is
interesting and provides a fitting commentary on the text.
If we pray for the coming of God's Kingdom we are also
praying that the Holy Spirit may enter into us. The
Reformers' interpretation of the second petition suggests
that they had taken account of this variant, and surely they
were right, but only if the words 'thy Kingdom' are understood to mean not a perfect Church but the end of the
whole present order and the advent of a new order of
existence. Happily, in the Kingdom of God there will be no
more need of the Church, for Jesus Christ will have completed what he has begun. We must still pray to God
because his cause is at stake. His commandments constantly
remind us of his patience towards us. During this anxious
time of his long-suffering, which we must endure before the
Kingdom comes, how necessary it is that God should utter
his word and sound the warning bell! Indeed, the end must
come! May God fulfil his promises and may we lay hold
of them as the promises of God. *Thy Kingdom come—this
Kingdom that has come already! Such is our prayer*—simple,
constant and very near to him.

5. *Thy Will be Done*

Now we return to the present which, like the past, is also the realm of God's will, the realm in which the plan is being carried out whereby he purposes to vindicate and glorify himself as Creator and Lord, and at the same time to vindicate and glorify his creature; that creature who, in comparison with him, is so small, so weak and in such peril, so prone to failure because he is stained with sin, lost, reduced to nothingness. But it is God's will to preserve and save his creature and to complete his work by the manifestation of his Kingdom.

May thy will . . . May the plan be carried out, may it be effective now, between the beginning and the end; may the time in which we live not pass by in vain. But this consummation cannot be achieved by us; we cannot carry out this will of God; his is the plan and its execution, his the time, both present and to come and all that time holds within it. Thus we are confronted for the third time with something to be prayed for : that God will deign to concern himself with us and with this world; that he will not cease to be patient, that he will reign even to the end. But, while we pray thus, we must recognize that it is being done, that God is engaged in carrying out his will and making it effective. We are praying to our Father in communion with Jesus Christ and therefore we know that his will is already done.

As in heaven . . . I hope I am not misinterpreting these words. *Thy will, Eternal God, is already done as thou hast intended it; it has been done, it will be done and it will work itself out in the course of time!* Before we speak, this will has been done where God is, in the mystery of what has taken place and is taking place in his presence. It was done in the creation, in his ordering of the world from the beginning; in the history of his covenant, which gives the true meaning of everything that has happened; that covenant as the prophets and apostles understood it, and the evidence of which is given us in Jesus Christ. *Thy will as it is known to thee, as it is seen by thine angels, as it exists 'at thy right hand', as we believe it to be although we do not see it, is done and is being done unceasingly in heaven.*

It is done as it ought to be done, with full understanding, without hindrance or frustration, in full liberty and so that grace reigns supreme and the creature responds in thankful recognition. Thus it is done in Jesus Christ; in heaven it is perfectly fulfilled. And this we believe and know by the word of Jesus Christ, whose spirit instructs us and assures us of it. His will has been done and is being done for ever.

There is, therefore, all the more reason to pray that it may be done *on earth* as it is in heaven; that it may be effective in our world and in our lives, so far as we can know it, veiled as it is; that the doing of his will on earth may follow the pattern of its execution in heaven. This means: may the light and shade, the mingling of secular and religious history, of saintliness and stupidity, of wisdom and vulgarity so characteristic of our existence, may all this confusion be cleared away! In heaven his will is perfectly done; then why not among us?

May this mingling of light and darkness not endure for ever; may we cease to misunderstand and oppose thy purposes; may we cease to contradict and constantly to misrepresent the Gospel so as to make it into a new law; may we give up behaving like bad servants; may we profit by thy patience and be converted instead of toying with a humanistic Christianity and a Christian humanism and continually provoking thy wrath afresh. In the execution of thy plan, deliver us from the endless imperfection of our obedience; come and set us free and extricate us at last from the contradictions by which we are beset, although we know that thy will is done and how it is done in heaven.

Once again, God's cause is at stake; and we are committed to his cause as he is to ours. His cause cannot be alien to us. We live in the present, within time; but time is very short, life goes by so quickly; there is not a moment to lose and we lose so many! What can be expected of the world if we Christians are so heedlessly earthly, so well satisfied with our imperfections, so much at ease when it should not be possible to be at ease. God reigns, and we pray that he will cause us to reign with him, no less.

6. *The Last Three Petitions*

Introductory remarks

First we should note a change of attitude in the second part of the Lord's Prayer, which begins with the request, *Give us*. In the first three petitions, although, while we pray, we are in some sort of relation with the heavenly Father, our prayer is like a sigh; we are dazzled by the majesty of that which fills our minds—the name, the kingdom, the will of God himself; we pray from afar, not daring to address him directly; 'may thy name, thy kingdom, thy will . . .' With the last three petitions we come to prayer properly speaking. But this change, though real, is, as we shall see, in keeping with the first three petitions.

Here two observations may be made :

1. The *us* of the 'Our Father' now becomes explicit and clearly heard. The words *our, we* or *us* occur eight times in these three verses. We may recall that the *us* of the Lord's Prayer is, so to speak, created by Christ's invitation and command : 'Follow me.' *We* are those who would learn to pray with Jesus Christ.

In this connexion four points may be noticed. (a) The *us* refers to the brotherhood of those who are with Jesus Christ, God and Man, who allows and commands them to join with him in his own intercession with God, that is, to pray with him. And (b), it is the *us* of the brotherhood which unites men to one another, even as they are united to Jesus Christ, by the same permission and commandment.

This brotherhood, however, is not a closed one; it is open inasmuch as it is involved with this world and represents it, including in that word 'world' those who have not yet heard and obeyed the Lord's invitation.

(c) The *us* of the last three petitions is that of a united community which thinks and acts as one body and knows, through profound experience, the wretchedness, of man's state. Nevertheless, in the midst of this wretchedness, of which it is well aware, this community is free to call on God in communion with Jesus Christ risen from the dead and with the common accord of its members, and to ask from our Father in heaven, the sovereign Creator, Lord, and Saviour, a complete and final deliverance, knowing that this Sovereign can and will grant it.

(d) It is the *us* of those who, being united with Jesus Christ crucified, are able to pray with him as members of God's family and, for that very reason, know, as no one else can, the extent of their own wretchedness and the wretchedness of the world, the depth of wickedness and the incurable sorrows of human existence, the downfall and ruin of God's good creation. They know that man cannot, by his own determination and his own efforts, extricate himself from this situation; they know that it is absolutely necessary to return to God and trust in him alone; in short, they realize the impossibility of living without God's free grace. Observe that *us* means those who, implicitly and silently, have already prayed the first three petitions concerned with God's cause and his glory. In the last three petitions the same people (*us*) put forward their own cause.

2. A second observation. Now, in these three petitions, prayer becomes explicit, direct, and insistent. It is one thing to pray: *May thy name . . . thy kingdom . . . thy will . . .* , and quite another to say: *Give us today . . . forgive us . . . lead us not . . . deliver us . . .* Note the boldness, I might even say the effrontery, of this demand.

Here is a man who dares to put God to the trouble of concerning himself with human affairs, who dares to issue orders; how can such a thing be? Our answer is: we are the only ones who are allowed, even commanded, in the first three petitions, to concern ourselves with God's affairs, with the hallowing of his name, the advent of his Kingdom, the doing of his will.

Is this our business? Certainly it is; we are permitted to concern ourselves with it. God has accepted us as fellow-workers (this is a biblical term); he has made his cause ours. And now, in consequence of those first three petitions, it is, so to speak, quite natural for us to call on God in the terms of the three petitions that follow. We are saying: *Our Father, behold us; thou seest us as we are and, it would seem, in the condition in which thou desirest to meet with us. We are concerned about thy cause* (assuming that we are in earnest in our prayer), *burning with the desire to see thy name hallowed. We have no other task; this is our care. There is no question of our being able to help ourselves; any such thought could only be faithlessness, disloyalty, disobedience. Therefore we place our lives in thy hands, who hast bidden us and commanded us to pray and to live for thy sake. Look on us, and do thou make our human cause thy care.*

Here is the source from which springs the audacity of these three petitions. They express this movement of thought: by asking God to give us what we need, both inwardly and outwardly, in order to live, we comply with his command to serve him for his glory.

In the first three petitions, Jesus Christ asks us to join him in his fight for God's cause and, at the same time, he invites us to join in his victory over the world and over everything which would prevent the realization of the longings expressed in those petitions. Jesus Christ has conquered and now he invites us to share in his victory. So that we may be free to utter those longings—May thy name . . .

thy Kingdom . . . thy will . . . we avail ourselves of
Christ's invitation to take part in his victory. Here is the
right and sufficient reason for what I have called the boldness and effrontery of that appeal: *Give us . . . forgive
us . . . ;* this is the reason for our daring to approach God
in this manner. For we must admit that this appeal is
astonishing; it cannot be made except in the freedom that
issues from our commitment as children of God and
brothers and sister of Jesus Christ.

These are the two essential aspects of what I have called
the change of attitude between the two parts of the Lord's
prayer. This change is, in fact, only the consequence of the
freedom which dominates the first part of the prayer.

We proceed now to the interpretation. We must not
forget, however, that any development can only be tenta-
tive. We shall follow the same order as before : first explaining the terms, then the way in which God answers and has
already answered this prayer, and finally we shall examine
the prayer itself.

We must remember that Luther and Calvin never ceased
emphasizing this point : that God has already heard us, and
that is why we are free, and are commanded, to pray. No
petition of the Lord's Prayer can be understood in any other
way.

7. *Our Daily Bread*

Some of the Reformers (and we can do likewise) included
in *our bread* everything we need to sustain life.

Those who are acquainted with Luther's Shorter Catechism will remember the well-known list that he draws up
to explain the meaning of the word *bread*: food, drink,
clothing, shoes, houses, farms, fields, land, money, property,
a good marriage, good children, good and trustworthy
authorities, a just government, favourable weather (neither
too hot nor too cold), health, honours, good friends, trusty
neighbours. This is no small order! The list shows us the
needs and the living conditions of a middle-class German

countryman of the sixteenth century. But nothing need prevent our interpreting and completing the list to suit the needs of our own time and our individual situations. It is certainly permissible to think of daily bread in this wider sense of the word. Nevertheless I would emphasize that it is advisable not to lose sight of the original, simple meaning of the word *bread*. In the language of the Bible *bread* is used in two senses:

1. That which is strictly necessary for life, the minimum nourishment which even the poor man cannot do without, the necessary minimum for the beggar and the tramp. It is the complement to the notion of *hunger*. Asking God to give us bread means appealing to his free grace which holds us and keeps us on the edge of the abyss of hunger and death. The minimum keeps us alive today; shall we have it tomorrow also? That is the vital question. Now we are living on it, but tomorrow? No one knows. We have no security if God does not give us this necessary bread, and with it life. The children of God know how precarious is our existence and the human situation in general. They know that, whether rich or poor, we are a people living in the wilderness, the people of Israel committed to God's cause. This is why we dare to ask him to preserve us from hunger and death, and we ask for it under this primitive form of *bread* because it cannot be taken for granted that we shall have it tomorrow.

2. In the Old and the New Testament *bread* is also the earthly symbol of God's eternal grace. Here the meaning of the word is at once more simple, natural and material as well as far more profound and sublime than we suppose. The natural and the sublime aspects are closely linked. They are a sign from God, given to this people in the wilderness, to the poor, the afflicted, to those who hunger and thirst, to those who are in the very jaws of death. Because of all that it stands for, bread is something sacred. Bread is the promise, and not simply the promise but also

the mystical presence of that food which nourishes for good and all; the food which, whosoever has eaten of it will not need to eat again. In the Bible every meal, the most frugal or the most sumptuous, is something sacred, for it is the promise of an eternal banquet. In the Bible the life of the body in this world is sacred because it is the promise of life immortal and eternal.

The word *bread*, as we have seen, is set beside the word *hunger*. But it also stands for that fullness of life which we shall experience in the new age, in the era which is to come. This actual bread which we eat is the pledge and the sign —and also the presence—of that fullness. This is what is called here *our bread*. Thus, *Give us our bread* means : give us what is necessary for the present and, at the same time, let it be to us a sign, a pledge given in advance, that we shall live. *According to thy promise, we, receiving it today, receive also the presence of thine everlasting goodness, the assurance that we shall live with thee.*

The word *daily* has been the subject of much discussion; it raises all kinds of questions and problems which I do not propose to deal with here. I shall simply suggest to you the most probable interpretation. *Epiousios* (daily) means, for each day, for the coming day. Give us today, give us each day, the bread we shall need tomorrow. We are living now, but shall we be alive next minute, next day? Will hunger and death spare us till then? This is the practical question which our precarious situation presents to us. You will remember that in Matthew 6, Jesus exhorts us not to be anxious about our life, what we shall eat or what we shall drink. Calvin was surely right to add, in his Commentary : it is very necessary to work for tomorrow's food. But neither anxiety nor work provides an answer to this question, Shall we be alive tomorrow? Prayer must take the place of anxiety and must underlie our work for the morrow. The children of God are not anxious about work; they work because they pray.

But perhaps at this point another meaning of the word *bread* should occur to us. Anxiety about the temporal tomorrow prefigures anxiety about the eternal tomorrow. For the uncertainty of this life is nothing compared to the uncertainty of human destiny. In the words of the requiem, 'What shall I say then, wretched man that I am?' May this fear be transformed and become a prayer! The children of God know the uncertainty of human life and everything we are afraid of in time and in eternity, but they hope to receive today, yes today, with their bread and in the form of earthly bread, the pledge, nay rather the first-fruits, of the bread which will feed them eternally, which will be their food in the eschatological tomorrow.

Let us now consider what this petition means. To ask God to give us bread, both earthly and heavenly, material and non-material, implies that we know God as the one who gives. We have already pointed out that to pray with full knowledge of the situation it is necessary to pray with the certainty of being heard; to pray at random, without this certainty, is not prayer at all. Our prayer, therefore, must begin with this implication.

Thou givest us our bread for the morrow, and thou givest it today. Thou art our faithful Creator, and never for one moment dost thou cease to be so. We are a people in the wilderness and yet encompassed by the splendours and riches of creation, by all thy creatures and by the covenant of grace which thou hast been pleased to establish between thyself and us. Thou desirest not our death, but our life.

On thy side, nothing whatever can be lacking. There is bread in plenty for us and for all who could join with us in this prayer, bread in plenty for everyone. There is no danger of our being overtaken by hunger or death. Thou art ready to preserve all those whom thou hast willed to call to the service of thy glory. Everything thou givest us is in truth the pledge of a living food, of that abundance in which we shall live for ever. This we know because thou

art our Father in heaven, our Father in Jesus Christ, with
whom we live and who has called us to follow him and
travel in his company: for the moment from afar, but
nevertheless we travel with him. And since thou art his
Father thou art ours also. Therefore we know that thou
hast prepared for us a meal, a banquet, both temporal and
eternal, and we hear thy voice bidding us to be guests at
thy table.

We need to hear that voice calling us, and we cannot
forget it: 'Come, for all things are ready.' This is what
impels us to pray and gives us leave to say to God: *Give us
today our daily bread.*

We must also say: *Do thou give it in such a way that it
is not given in vain but that we may truly receive that
bread which thou has prepared at thy table in the Holy
Communion; that we may take from thy hands the bread
which thou hast created for us and dost give us. Help us,
therefore, and enlighten us, lest at the very moment when
thou givest us afresh that ineffable and incomparable gift
of thy patience and our hope, we should bear ourselves like
gluttons or men surfeited with food; see to it that we do
not squander or destroy that gift. Grant that each one may
receive his bread without dispute or quarrelling. If anyone
has more than he needs, grant him the knowledge that he
is thereby appointed a servant and minister of thy grace, to
be used in thy service and the service of others; and may
all who are in special danger from hunger, death, and from
the chances of mortal life find brothers and sisters whose
eyes and ears are open and who are alive to their responsibilities. How shameful is our ingratitude and our social
injustice! How senseless it is that in the midst of men who
are surrounded by thy gifts and swollen with riches, there
should still be some who are perishing from hunger!*

*See to it that we receive the food we need and that we
receive it as thou givest it, that is, as a sign and a promise;
and as we enjoy that sign, and as we bless thee ('Bless the*

Lord, O my soul, and forget not all his benefits'), may we enjoy in anticipation the things thou dost promise us, so that even now we may take part in that feast at which thou wilt preside from everlasting to everlasting.

As you see, there is good reason to pray. Indeed it is our cause that is at stake. We are completely dependent on God, and truly he must make our cause his own so that it may be sustained and be victorious. We are in the position of being free to call on him without fear, in the certain knowledge that he hears us, and that he has always done and always will do what we ask of him.

8. Forgive Us Our Debts

We are in default in our relations with God; we owe him a debt which we have not paid, and if we are unable to pay we continue to be defaulters; if one fails to meet one's obligations, one is in default. One may be righteous, but nevertheless one is guilty. The result is that we offend the person in relation to whom we are at fault.

We are debtors to God; we owe him not any special thing, whether it be little or much, but quite simply ourselves, all we are, creatures sustained and nourished by his goodness. We, his children, called by his word to serve and glorify him, brothers of the man Jesus Christ, we fall short of what we owe to God. What we are and what we do bear no relation to what we have been given. We are his children and we are unable to recognize the fact. Calvin writes: 'Whosoever will not confess that we offend God like debtors who do not pay, shuts himself out from Christianity.' And Luther: 'Before God everyone is forced to lower his plumes.' Thus Christianity recognizes this state of things, but we are powerless to put it right. Even while, in response to his invitation, we are trying to obey and do what he requires of us, we allow our own ideas, our own leanings, our morality and religion to intrude, and we are continually obliged to recognize afresh that we are not worthy to serve him; and when we look at ourselves we know that we are without hope before him.

For even while we are living as Christians we are increasing our debt to him and making our desperate situation worse from day to day. And I think that as one grows older one realizes more and more the hopelessness of our position. Things go from bad to worse. We meet a rebuff at the very beginning of the Lord's Prayer where we are faced with this question: How have we the effrontery to draw near to God? We are zealous for his cause and straightway lay our own needs before him; who are we to claim to be God's fellow-workers? and then to say to him: Attend to me, to us! Give us! We who have offended against him! Again everything seems to be called in question.

What does *forgive* mean? Ideally it means to regard one's debtor as having done one no wrong, not to impute his fault to him, or hold his guilt against him, though he himself is aware of it and recognizes it. It means to let him start again with a clean sheet, to give him another chance. Forgive us! This petition excludes any sort of claim on our part, it denies us any right, even the slightest, to demand anything whatever from God. Neither man's fault nor man himself as defaulter can be excused; man is unforgivable. He has no right to claim the remission of his debt. The right to restore the guilty to their place as children of God belongs solely to him whom we have wronged; it is the right of the creditor or the sovereign, of that King to whom we have been disloyal, in whose service we have been, and always are, defaulters; that right can only pertain to the free mercy of God. We ask of God, then, that he will be pleased to use on our behalf that right which lies in his grace. We can trust in him. But unless we renounce completely any right whatever on our part, we shall not know how to pray as is fitting.

As we also forgive those who have offended against us.

Is this a sort of preliminary condition which we lay down for ourselves in order to obtain forgiveness from God? No, it is rather a necessary criterion by which we may understand God's forgiveness. For anyone who knows that he is handed over to the mercy of God, that he cannot live without Divine forgiveness, anyone who has lived through such an experience, cannot do otherwise than forgive those who have offended against him (we are all offenders, we are all debtors one to another all the time). And even if the debts of our debtors seem very large, they are always infinitely less than those we owe to God. How can we hope for God's forgiveness, we whose debts are so great, if we are not willing to do this small thing—forgiving those who have offended against us? Having such a hope for oneself must surely open one's heart and soften one's feelings and one's judgment in regard to others. There is no merit, no moral effort or virtue in being able to forgive. How irritating those people are who, perpetually smiling, pursue you with their forgiveness!

Human forgiveness is a lovely thing and almost a physical necessity. In the light of the Divine forgiveness, when we look on those poor souls who have offended against us, even the worst cases seem not very serious; let us not settle down and take pleasure in the offences which have been committed against us; let us preserve a sense of humour about them, and let us freely make this small gesture of forgiveness towards those others. There is no occasion to regard this as part of the Christian warrior's moral armour; it is not a helmet or a sword which could endow us with courage and strength, but something which ought to be quite natural. Anyone who does not exercise this small amount of freedom is beyond the reach of Divine forgiveness; it might be said of him that he does not know how to pray and thus can receive nothing. This is no exhortation to go and forgive others, but a plain declaration that the Divine forgiveness received by a man makes him able to forgive. God's forgiveness operates on the divine plane and cannot be compared with what happens on the human level; nevertheless it is necessary that this small matter of forgiving our debtors should be practised on the human level. How can I hope for something myself if I will not give even this to my neighbour? I cannot escape from the obligation of giving this small fragment! But by this action I shall not make myself worthy to receive God's forgiveness : I shall simply prove the sincerity of my hope and my prayer.

We must clearly understand the nature of God's forgiveness; it is in no sense an uncertain hope or an ideal to be sought or imagined; it is a fact. Before I ask for it, God has already bestowed forgiveness. He who does not know this, prays to no purpose. Forgiveness is ours already; that is the reality by which we live.

Our Father who art in heaven, truly thou hast forgiven our transgressions. Before I say to thee 'Forgive me', thou hast established and proclaimed thy right to pardon, the righteousness of thy mercy, thy right to overlook our faults and not to regard us as offenders. In the person of thy Son, thou, the holy and righteous God, hast changed places with us, perfidious and unrighteous men. Thou hast put thyself in our place so that order may be restored in our favour. Thou hast obeyed and suffered for us, thou hast destroyed our sin and the sins of all mankind. And this thou hast done once for all.

Thou hast annulled those sins which are with us from our birth to our death, and also those which we commit each day, every moment in one way or another; those sins which we know only too well, and others that we are not aware of, but which will be revealed one day when our account is made up. Then we shall see ourselves as thou seest us. Thou hast abolished all these trangressions and hast begotten a new man (a new 'us' and a new 'me'), without sin, without transgression, a man who is pleasing to thee, righteous in thine eyes, pure and spotless and with out reproach. Thou hast begotten this man and hast gathered us round him, round the cross of thy Son, so that we may be witnesses of our own judgment, because we must indeed enter into this judgment and this death which he has suffered in our stead to set us free.

Thou hast given us thy Holy Spirit so that this new man which thou hast created in Jesus Christ may live in us, and thy grace, revealed in him, may become ours. Because thou hast done this great work in thy Son and through thy Holy Spirit, we are not permitted to remain any longer in doubt and uncertainty and anxiety on account of our transgressions; henceforth our sins are thy concern, not ours. Thou dost forbid us to look backward, to feel ourselves crushed and, as it were, chained to our past or to what we are and do today or even tomorrow.

The time for fixing our eyes always on our sins instead of on thee is past; thou hast cut us off from the past. In Jesus Christ thou hast made of me a new creature and dost allow me, and command me, to look forward. Not that we are to make light of what we are and do, or what we have been and have done, nor are we to put our trust in what we shall be or do. On the contrary, we are to be always on our guard, knowing that we are being and shall be judged, but also trusting in thee and in what thou hast done, in the judgment thou hast pronounced and the death thou hast suffered for our sakes. This is something which has been completed. But this action, already completed, has secured for us a future, and we have only to walk on the path which lies open before us. Thy forgiveness has made us free to take that path.

We must, however, thoroughly understand that we cannot in all seriousness speak to God in this way or receive his forgiveness without praying 'Forgive us our debts'. Now it is for us to move towards that perfect future; it is for us to believe and to make effective the new beginning inaugurated by the death of Jesus Christ.

May we now live our life as it really is, that is to say, united with his, taking the place that he has given us, the place where we really are, where he suffered and obeyed and lived for us. May we put on that new man begotten by God in Christ; may we cease to live heedlessly, and live henceforth in the reality of what God has done for us; may we not withstand the Holy Spirit when he assures us that we are thy children, not on account of our merits but because of thy free pardon, because thou hast conquered sin the flesh and hast exalted thy poor creatures as high as the heavens. May thy forgiveness sanctify us more and more, in spite of what we have been and still are and will be. We know that we shall be sanctified with the holiness that is thine, and that it will triumph over our wretchedness and all our impurities. Oh may thy forgiveness sanctify us for that day when, at the second coming of thy Son, thou wilt reveal to us for the last time, in the light of thy presence, all our shortcomings, our depravity, our transgressions, and everything we have concealed! But, much more than this, thou wilt reveal thy right to pardon, the righteousness of thy mercy which has prevailed over our wretchedness. Forgive us; grant us today, and through the days to come, which your long-suffering may allow us, to live in the liberty of the pardon thou hast given.

Indeed, we have reason to pray! And if we consider the forgiveness we are bound to extend to others, how much more keenly shall we feel the need to pray. For if we refuse to make this gesture we are far from having apprehended the Divine forgiveness.

Thus, in this fifth petition, we confess our bankruptcy, and anyone who is unwilling to do so, must give up asking God to forgive him. We must recognize that our own cause is lost, but if we do, it will become victorious for us, for then it rests in the hands of him who has forgiven and still forgives.

9. *Deliver Us from the Evil One*

Lead us not into temptation. Here we are concerned with the great testing, not with evil merely, but with the Evil One.

There are minor trials, sins which are not mortal, one might almost call them provisional temptations, which God sends us every day and which vary according to our age: some for the young, some for the not so young, and some for the old. God sends them because they are necessary for us; they are temptations which we can resist. In the Epistle of James, indeed, it is written that they can be an occasion of joy: 'Blessed is the man that endureth temptation' (Jas. 1.12). There are evils which cause suffering, both within and without, that may be severe and extremely unwelcome; but when looked at closely, they are found to be bearable. It can even be said, as Paul does, that 'they work together for the good of those who love God' (Rom. 8.28). One must not ask to be spared these trials and evils at all costs. It would be wrong to say to God: *Do not make me go through what Job, David and all the saints have had to endure, in accordance with thy purpose which is always good.* We are wrong to cry: *Deliver us from everything which might be a danger or a cause of sorrow to us.* The sixth petition of the 'Our Father' is not concerned with evils of this kind, minor trials which are only relative and can be endured.

But there is the great eschatological testing,[1] which may, no doubt, appear in the guise of a minor trial, but is itself entirely different: it is the activity of the Evil One. Moral and physical testings may in fact be identified with it; they can be the expression of its deadly action, but a distinction must be drawn. There is no question here of an ordinary danger which could be clearly recognized and resisted; it is,

[1] The 'temptation' (NEB: 'test') of which the Lord's Prayer speaks is generally agreed by scholars to refer to the testing of man in the final conflict with evil.—Ed.

rather, the infinitely dangerous threat of that nothingness
that is opposed to God himself. It is a threat which involves,
for the creature, not merely a temporary danger, a relatively
unimportant destruction, or a momentary corruption, but
complete and utter ruin and final extinction.

This is the supreme testing. There is nothing in it from
which we may profit; it is fruitless, and if it comes upon us,
one cannot say of it, 'rejoice'; it holds no hope. There is an
intolerable, unendurable evil which is in no way a rival to
what is good, and the threat of it exists and manifests its
presence. This supreme and infinite evil is not part of the
created order. There are evils belonging to the created order,
as we have said, but they are relative and can be borne.
But that evil has no part in what God has willed and
created; it exists at the farthest limit of creation, on the left
hand as God is himself the limit on the right. This absolute
evil thrusts itself upon the created order in forms which we
all recognize—sin and death. It is seen in the unlawful and
inexplicable domination of what the Scripture calls the
Devil. The creature is defenceless in face of this menace;
God is stronger than it, but his creatures are not. Once the
Devil has gained a footing he wreaks endless havoc, against
which we can do nothing without God's protection. Where
God is not, or where he is not master, there the Devil
reigns: no other alternative exists.

The Reformers, both Luther and Calvin, experienced not
only small trials but the great testing; they knew that they
had to do with the Evil One. They had no respect for him,
since he is not worthy of respect, but they were aware of
his existence; they knew very well that they had to reckon
not with men's malice only—that of the Pope and all those
who opposed them; there is also the Evil One, who turns to
evil all those things with which we are occupied and about
which we care. God's enemy is the enemy of his creatures
also. If we are to pray this last petition as we should, we
must recognize that the Reformers were right.

I have no intention of preaching to you about the Devil; one cannot preach him and I have no desire to cause you pain. But, nevertheless, this is something real, which modern Christians tend to pass over too lightly. There is an enemy possessed of superior power whom we cannot resist without God's help. I have no love for demonology nor for the way people concern themselves with it nowadays in Germany and possibly elsewhere also. Do not, therefore, ask me questions about demons, for I am no expert! We should, however, realize that the Devil exists and then make all haste to get away from him.

We pray thee, our Father, so to lead us that we may be able to avoid this sinister, this baleful borderland; lead us thy children, the redeemed of Jesus Christ. Spare us, not the struggle, for we must accept it, nor suffering, for one must suffer, but spare us the encounter with that enemy who is stronger than our utmost strength, more wily than our understanding (including our understanding of theology), *more dangerously sentimental* (for the Devil is sentimental too!) *than we can ever be. He is more pious* (yes, the Devil is pious also) *than our Christian piety, ancient, modern or theological. Shield us from the possibility of such evil, from which we should not know how to protect ourselves and which would utterly and finally brutalize us.*

This is not merely one trial among others, if somewhat more painful or sinister; it is the supreme testing in which the impossible becomes possible.

Deliver us from the Evil One. We discover and experience his power, though in fact the power is apparent and not real. But the terrible thing is that, though unreal, it is active; it is useless to make little of it because it is unreal; it is dangerous because it is a crafty and insidious power and its domination is only too real. Our sins give it power over us because we have yielded to it. We are in the very jaws of death; we complain, we suffer, but we cannot free ourselves.

The Greek word usually translated 'deliver' may also be rendered 'snatch' us from those jaws. In the Old Testament, the Psalms from beginning to end echo with the cry 'snatch us', and Christianity takes up this cry in the sixth petition, for it knows this enemy because it knows Christ and that he has encountered not only the ill-will of men but also the enemy of God and of his creature. It needed the Son of God to unmask the sinister wickedness of the enemy. This is why the Lord's Prayer ends with this cry *de profundis*, and if our prayer does not end on this same note, it does not answer to what Christ has taught us.

But this last petition also presupposes that we know, more certainly than we know anything else about this danger, that God has already done what we ask of him; before we thought of praying or had framed this petition : *lead us not into temptation*, he had done it. In truth, God does not drive us into this testing.

No, our Father, this thou dost not do; how couldst thou, who hast revealed thyself in thy Son? Thou dost not deceive us; thy mind concerning this great testing is not in doubt, it is explicit; thy resistance is clear and plain and has been so since the first day of Creation when thy word was uttered: 'Let there be light.' Thou, our Father, hast no commerce with evil, thou knowest no compromise, thou dost not tolerate it. The menace of nothingness can never come from thee, it will never be admitted or allowed by thee. Nay, rather, when thou leadest us in thy paths, in the way of thy goodness and thy forgiveness, thou wilt lead us always to the right, never to the left. We can be certain that while we follow thy word we shall never be led into the great testing. While we follow the path that thou hast prepared for us and hast revealed in thy Son we shall always be sheltered from this aberration. Thou wilt deliver us from the Evil One.

Art thou not God the liberator? There is only one who is able to effect a decisive deliverance, and thou art he. We

*know now that thou art the great liberator; thou thyself
hast joined issue with the Evil One, that usurper whose
dominion must be destroyed because he has no part in thy
creation. Thou hast gone forth to shatter the powers of
this kingdom of the Devil; thou hast caused him to fall
like lightning from heaven, and we have seen him fall.
In the resurrection of thy Son thou hast triumphed
over the powers of darkness; thou hast proclaimed thy
victory by many signs and wonders, and thou dost proclaim it still among us by baptism in the name of thy Son
and by the presence of his body and his blood in the Holy
Communion.*

*Thou hast snatched us already from those jaws; thine be
the glory! We need no longer be oppressed by the menace
of the Evil One or go in fear of him. That is why we pray
'lead us not into temptation, but deliver us from the Evil
One'. Be ever with us, O thou our true and faithful guide,
to show us the right path and open it before our feet; thou
art the victorious leader before whom the Evil One is no
more than a witless and ludicrous goblin, a nothing.*

*We know that without thee it would not be so. Our ways
would not be the right way, and our moral and religious
enterprises could never be successful. Without thee our
efforts to overcome temptation, evil and the Devil would
only make matters worse. It is for thee alone to protect us
and rescue us from the position we are in. Once more, to
thee be the glory, to thee in whom we put our trust. This is
the final liberty that God grants us.*

There is reason to pray. Without the last petition of the
'Our Father', and the response which precedes our prayer,
we should be not merely crippled and handed over to
judgment, but reduced to nothingness. *Thine be the glory!
Thou hast destroyed the one who would have destroyed us!
Thou hast loved us and dost love us, and thy love is
efficacious; it delivers once and for all!*

10. *The Doxology*

Of this we shall speak only briefly. The words: *for thine is the kingdom, the power, and the glory for ever and ever,* do not belong to the original text of the Gospel; it is generally agreed that they are not authentic. The doxology is an addition, an extension, introduced for the liturgical use of the Lord's Prayer. The whole congregation would say, or sing, these words as a response to each of the six petitions said by the priest. But this does not prevent our considering the meaning of these words. What were the thoughts of the people in the Church of the second century when, at the end of the Lord's Prayer, this doxology was spoken? It is possible to see a connexion with the sixth petition; *deliver us from the Evil One.* In fact, of course, the kingdom, the power and the glory belong to God, not to the devil, sin, death, or hell. *For* means: we ask thee to deliver us from the Evil One, because to thee belong the kingdom, the power and the glory. Or, in other words: Show thyself to be the King, powerful and glorious, by delivering us from the Evil One.

There is another explanation which does not necessarily exclude the first. These last words embrace the whole prayer; the underlying idea would then be: *It is necessary for us to pray because the kingdom, the power, and the glory belong to thee and not to us, or to Christian men, or to the pious. All the things we ask of thee can be done only by thee, and this is why we call upon thee.* The Heidelberg Catechism explains it thus: *Thou art our King, the Almighty, who can and will give us all good things so that thy name may be glorified and not ours, nor the name of Christianity, nor that of the Church.*

Amen. It will be enough to recall the words of Luther and of the Heidelberg Catechism. Luther asserts that it is a good thing to say *Amen*! In other words, to learn not to doubt when we pray but to believe, because *Amen* means 'So be it!' Prayer is not an undertaking left to chance, a voyage into the blue. It must end as it began with conviction : Yes, may it be so!

The Heidelberg Catechism declares that *Amen* means that the certainty of the divine response is greater than our own certainty concerning our needs and our desires. Not what we ask is the most certain thing in our prayers, but what comes from God : his response.

IV

PREFACE TO PREACHING

1. *Some Personal Words* (1961)

A NUMBER of my writings, hitherto unpublished even in German, have on occasion been privately circulated; among these is a course of lectures—I no longer remember when or where they were delivered—on 'Preaching and how to prepare it'.

It will be apparent that here I have ventured into the field of practical theology, and if this little book should come to the notice of experts in that discipline, they will, I trust, forgive the liberty I have taken and judge it not too severely.

With regard to the dogmatic elements in these lectures, it should be remembered that when they were given I was still a comparatively young man; since that time, with advancing age I have perhaps advanced in wisdom also—at least I hope so. However that may be, so far as dogma is concerned there is nothing of importance that I wish to retract, nor are there any changes that I wish to make in the text presented here.

Moreover, anyone who is acquainted with my *Dogmatics* will recognize at once that the views expressed there are essentially the same as those of this earlier work, though argued and formulated in slightly different terms.

The present work is primarily concerned with certain practical rules and suggestions which I still hold to be essential and worth considering—or at least of being read carefully and discussed. Anyone, of course, is free to criticise them.

A well-informed young theologian might find it of

interest to compare some of my sermons—for example those in the series *Deliverance to the Captives*,[1] or simply the three outlines suggested in this book—with the principles expounded here; and see how closely I have adhered to them.

2. *Basic Definitions*

This study is an expansion of two definitions:

1. *Preaching is the Word of God which he himself has spoken; but God makes use, according to his good pleasure, of the ministry of a man who speaks to his fellow men, in God's name, by means of a passage from Scripture. Such a man fulfils the vocation to which the Church has called him and, through his ministry, the Church is obedient to the mission entrusted to her.*

2. *Preaching follows from the command given to the Church to serve the Word of God by means of a man called to this task. It is this man's duty to proclaim to his fellow men what God himself has to say to them, by explaining, in his own words, a passage from Scripture which concerns them personally.*

The reason for making these two statements is that preaching has a dual aspect: the Word of God and human speech.

In attempting to describe, in theological terms, what happens when a man preaches, one can only give indications and suggest points of reference. We are carried beyond human thinking to God, who utters the first and the last word. God cannot be enclosed in any human concept; he lives and acts by his own sovereign power.

The theologian has to move in two directions; his thought must ascend and also descend. And even when this has been done, he fulfils his duty of proclaiming the Word of God only in a partial and imperfect manner. But if he carries

[1] Sermons translated for the SCM Press in 1961. Most were preached in Basel Prison, which Dr Barth has been visiting regularly—Ed.

C

out this task aright he can be certain of doing what has to
be done and what he ought to do.

His discourse is his own; it is neither reading nor
exegesis. He utters the Word which he has heard in the
Scriptures, as he himself has received it. His calling as a
preacher is comparable, in a sense, to that of the apostles.
He also has, but on another plane, a prophetic function.

The attempt to serve the Word of God and to proclaim
it is a duty laid on the Church. The most appropriate word
in this connexion is *Ankündigung* (announcing what is to
come) rather than *Verkündigung* (describing what is). God
will make himself heard; he it is who speaks, not man. The
preacher only has to announce the fact that God is about
to speak. The word *Ankündigung* does not imply that the
hearer is called to make a decision. A decision, if it is made,
is a matter between the individual and God alone and is
not a necessary element in preaching.

This does not mean, however, that preaching is never a
call to action. In fact it is, precisely, a call addressed to the
believing Church. But a decision is the work of divine grace
—or rather of that mystery which is the direct encounter
between man and God. The preacher must recognize that
the decision does not depend on him.

It should be added that there is no basis in human experience for the concept of preaching. It is a purely
theological concept resting on faith alone. As has been said,
it is directed to one end only : to point to divine truth. It
cannot pass beyond the bounds of its own nature, to assume
another form more easy to grasp.

V

ESSENTIAL CHARACTERISTICS
OF PREACHING

1. *Preaching and Revelation*

THE RELATION of preaching to revelation may be considered first in its negative aspect. It is not the function of the preacher to reveal God or to act as his intermediary. When the Gospel is preached God speaks: there is no question of the preacher revealing anything or of a revelation being conveyed through him. It is necessary, in all circumstances, to have regard to the fact that God has revealed himself (Epiphany) and will reveal himself (*Parousia*). Whatever happens by means of preaching—in the interval between the first and the second coming—is due to its divine subject. Revelation is a closed system in which God is the subject, the object and the middle term.

The practical consequences of this are as follows:

(a) Preaching cannot claim to convey the truth of God; neither can its aim be to provide a rational demonstration of the existence of God by expounding briefly or at length certain theoretical propositions. There is no proof that God exists except that which he himself provides. Nor are we required to display the truth of God in an artistic form by the use of vain images or by presenting Jesus Christ in outpourings of sentimental eloquence. When Paul told the Galatians that he had portrayed before their eyes Jesus Christ crucified, he was not referring to speeches in which he had used every device of artistry to capture the imagination of his hearers. For him, to portray Christ was to show him forth in plain truth without embellishments. We are

under orders to 'make no image or likeness'. Since God wills
to utter his own truth, his Word, the preacher must not
adulterate that truth by adding his own knowledge or art.
From this point of view, the representation of the figure of
Christ in art, and the crucifix in churches, may be of
doubtful value, as may be symbolic images of God.

(b) Neither must the preacher seek to establish the reality
of God. His task is to build God's Kingdom and he must
work towards a decision. His message must be authentic
and alive; he must lay bare man's actual situation and con-
front him with God. But he is going too far if he thinks of
this confrontation as 'a sickness which leads to death'
(Kierkegaard). This phrase no doubt presupposes things
which are implicit in preaching, but it concerns the action
of God and no man ought to intrude in what is not his
province.

If it is maintained that a preacher ought to convert others
and cause his hearers to share his own faith, this can only
be understood in the sense that he should be aware of what
is happening when he is bearing witness. The preacher who
believes in Christ will never present himself to his congregation in such a way that they will suppose him able to
bestow on them Christ and the Spirit, or think that the
initiative in what is done is his. God is not superfluous, a
Deus otiosus; he is the author of what is done. We can act
only in obedience to the task given to us; neither our aims
nor our methods are of our own devising.

Our preaching does not differ in essence from that of the
prophets and apostles who 'saw and touched'; the difference
is due to the different historical setting in which it takes
place. The prophets and apostles lived during that moment
of the historical revelation of which Scripture is the record.
We, on the other hand, bear witness to the Revelation.

But if God speaks through our words then in fact that
same situation is produced : the prophets and apostles are
present even though the words are spoken by an ordinary

minister. But we must not think of ourselves as uttering prophecies; if Christ deigns to be present when we are speaking, it is precisely because that action is God's, not ours. Since this is the way things happen, the preacher can make no claims for his own programme.

Thus any independent undertaking that is attempted, whether with the intention of developing a theoretical subject, or with the practical purpose of leading one's hearers into a certain frame of mind, can in fact be nothing else but a waiting on God, so that he may do with it what he will. If the preacher sets himself to expound a particular idea, in some form or another—even if the idea is derived from a serious and well-informed exegesis—then the Scripture is not allowed to speak for itself; the preacher is discoursing on it. To put it more positively, preaching should be an explanation of Scripture; the preacher does not have to speak 'on' but 'from' (*ex*), drawing from the Scriptures whatever he says. He does not have to invent but rather to repeat something. No thesis, no purpose derived from his own resources must be allowed to intervene: God alone must speak. Perhaps, afterwards, he will have to ask himself whether he has allowed himself to be influenced by an idea of his own or has attempted to arrive at a unity which only God could create. He must follow the special trend of his text, and keep to it wherever it may lead him, not raising questions about a subject which may, as it seems to him, arise from the text.

In this connexion it may be pointed out that the choice of a text may present dangers, in that one may choose a text because it bears on a subject one would like to discuss; one may even turn to the Bible in order to find in it something which fits in with one's own thoughts! To have to speak from a particular text to a particular congregation in an actual situation is in itself a dangerous undertaking. It may be that in that situation God will speak and work a miracle, but we must not build on that miracle in advance.

Otherwise it would be easy for a preacher to become a sort of Pope, and indoctrinate his congregation with his own ideas by presenting them as the Word of God.

The positive aspect of this matter must now be considered. The starting point is the fact that God wills to reveal himself; he himself bears witness to his Revelation; he has effected it and will effect it. Thus preaching takes place in obedience, by listening to the will of God. This is the process in which the preacher is involved, which constitutes part of his life and controls the content as well as the form of his preaching. Preaching is not a neutral activity, nor yet a joint action by two collaborators. It is the exercise of sovereign power on the part of God and obedience on the part of man.

Only when preaching is controlled by this relationship can it be regarded as *kerygma* or Gospel, that is, as news proclaimed by a herald who thereby fulfils his function. Then the preacher is omnipotent, but only because of the omnipotence of the one who has commissioned him. The *kerygma* means therefore to start from the Epiphany of Christ in order to move towards the Day of the Lord. Thus New Testament preaching consists in a dual movement: God has revealed himself, God will reveal himself.

From these considerations certain consequences follow:

(a) *The fixed point from which all preaching starts* is the fact that God has revealed himself, and this means that the Word has become flesh; God has assumed human nature; in Christ he has put on fallen humanity. Man, who is lost, is called back to his home. The death of Christ is the final term of the Incarnation. In him our sin and our punishment are put away, they no longer exist; in him man has been redeemed once for all; in him God has been reconciled with us. To believe means to see and know and recognize that this is so.

If then preaching is dominated by this starting point, the preacher can adopt no attitude other than that of a man to whom everything is given. He knows, without any possible doubt, that everything has been restored by God himself. He is, however, constantly beset by the temptation to denounce man's sin or to attack his errors. Certainly it is necessary to speak of human sin and error, but only in order to show that sin is annihilated and error destroyed. For either it is true that man is forgiven or else there is no forgiveness whatever. Sin cannot be spoken of except as borne by the Lamb of God.

At the same time, to separate the Gospel from the Law in preaching is not Christian. How is it possible to proclaim the Gospel without also hearing the Law which says: 'Thou shalt fear and love God'? This error is particularly astonishing in Calvinism.

Moreover, from its first to its last word, preaching follows a movement. This has nothing to do with the preacher's convictions, or his earnestness or his zeal. The movement starts from the fact that the Word became flesh, and the preacher must abandon himself to its guidance. If this rule were observed, how many introductory remarks would become quite unnecessary! The movement does not consist so much in going towards men as in coming from Christ to meet them. Preaching therefore proceeds downwards; it should never attempt to reach up to a summit. Has not everything been done already?

(b) It has already been pointed out that preaching has one single point of departure, which is that God has revealed himself. It should also be recognized that it has *one unique end*: the fulfilment of the Revelation, the redemption which awaits us.

From beginning to end the New Testament looks towards the achievement of salvation; this, however, is not to deny that all has been accomplished once for all. The Christ who has come is the one who will return. The life of faith is orientated towards the day of the coming (*Parousia*). The point of departure and the point to which everything tends

are summed up in the declaration : 'Christ the same yesterday, today, and forever'. And assuming that we await the
whole Christ, christology and eschatology may be said to
be one. Revelation, therefore, is before as well as behind us.

It follows, then, that preaching moves in an atmosphere
of expectation. There is no settling down comfortably in
faith and the assurance of salvation, as if divine grace
manifested in the past allowed us now to take our rest in
tranquillity. Without doubt there is a profound and joyful
assurance, but there is also the solemn and earnest concern
of one who watches because the end is near. Preaching, like
all Christian life, grows to its fullness between the first
Advent and the second.

We walk by faith, not by sight (II Cor. 5.7); if in this
present time we were living by sight, we should have
nothing to wait for; there would be neither yesterday nor
tomorrow. But we live by faith, that is to say, we come
from Christ and are going to Christ. Peace and joy abound
on either hand, but on this journey we go from riches to
destitution and from destitution to new riches. The preacher
must show the real nature of this journey in faith; that is
to say he must make it clear that confident assurance is not
Christian unless it is shot through with longing for a salvation yet to be realized in its fullness in Christ. Christ has
come, Christ will come again and we await the day of his
coming : this is the word of command. 'The Word was
made flesh' has as its response : 'Amen, come quickly, Lord
Jesus'.

The Lutheran tendency is to confine itself to what is past,
and for this reason its preaching is always liable to be biased
towards dogmatism and religious experience. But Phil. 3
refers to Phil. 2; having described the Christian vocation,
the Apostle declares : 'Not that I have already attained . . .
but I press on . . .' There is movement even in the tranquillity of faith. The preacher must proclaim with conviction that 'all has been done' but also that 'all must be

changed'. We look for a new heaven and a new earth. We know, indeed, that we are reconciled with God, but we still await the fulfilment of the promise : 'See, I make all things new'. That is why preaching rests entirely on hope, for the Christian 'now' is simply the passage from yesterday to tomorrow, from Epiphany to *Parousia*. From this point of view we are a people that walk in darkness, but we see a great light; 'the night is far spent, the day is at hand'. If the preacher's message is to conform to Revelation, these two fixed points must be kept in mind.

2. *Preaching and the Church*

Preaching has its place within the context of what is called the Church; it is bound up with the Church's existence and its mission. Precisely for this reason, preaching must conform to Revelation. But it should be noted that Revelation is set in the framework of the Old and New Testaments and is, therefore, a particular, concrete event taking place at a specific period in history; it is not an idea of general significance which could arise at any time or in any place. Consequently preaching is not concerned with aspects of human existence in its natural state or with the progress of its history; it is not inspired by any philosophy or conceptual view of life and the world; its subject is solely that particular event, the gift of God in the context of history.

Again it must be emphasized that preaching is not man's attempt to add something to Revelation; the movement which proceeds from the first to the second Advent is not initiated by man but is due simply to the action of God's grace. God draws near to men; men cannot, by their own efforts, rise to win for themselves what God has appointed for them.

The task of the preacher can therefore be summed up thus : to reproduce in thought that one unique event, the gift of God's grace. If once he has recognized the impossibility of doing otherwise, then he will see clearly that no philosophical, political, or aesthetic considerations can influence his choice of a field for his activity. In the nature of things there can be only one—the Church.

There a relationship exists which is prior to anything we know on earth—whether of family, society, nation or race; and the nature of that relationship is entirely different from that of the created order. In the Church, where the Word of reconciliation rings out, all other relationships are seen to be stained with impurities, contaminated, submerged in a fallen world and, as such, lying under the stroke of judgment. But the same Word also assures us that our sickness is healed and the whole burden of the consequences of sin is carried away. Moreover, in the Word of reconciliation there is also the message of Creation.

Preaching, when it is true to what God has revealed to us, effects reconciliation; and wherever men receive this Word, there is the Church, the assembly of those who have been called by the Lord. Not general reflections on man and the cosmos but Revelation is the only legitimate ground for preaching. Because this call is sounded and men are able to hear it, the Church exists. Thus the bond which links preaching to the Church results directly from its faithfulness to Revelation.

The foregoing considerations will become clearer if two points are emphasized. The true Church is characterized by the fact that 'the pure Word of God is preached, and the Sacraments be duly ministered'.[1] These two concepts, sacraments and preaching the Gospel, throw light on the connexion between the Church and conformity to Revelation.

The sacrament, with all its wealth of meaning, may first be considered, for it is impossible to understand what

---

[1] The translation in Article 19 in the Church of England's 39 Articles, of Article 7 of Lutheranism's Augsburg Confession of 1530, quoted by Dr Barth.—Ed.

preaching is without understanding what the sacrament is. There is indeed no preaching, in the precise meaning of the term, except when it is accompanied and illuminated by the sacrament. What is the sacrament? Unlike preaching or any other ecclesiastical activity, the sacrament goes back to that action of the Revelation which founded the Church and constitutes her promise, for the sacrament is not merely a word but an action, physically and visibly performed.

Baptism confers on a man the seal of belonging to the Church, for his life begins not with his birth but with his baptism. To be baptized means that a relationship between the Revelation and a man has been established and is made actual in a specific situation (Rom. 6.3). If baptism represents the event which is the point of departure, the Lord's Supper, on the other hand, is the sign of the same event but turned towards the future which we all await (I Cor. 11.26).

Preaching, then, is given within that Church where the sacrament of grace and the sacrament of hope are operative; but each partakes at once of the character of grace and hope for neither sacrament nor preaching has significance except within the Church, where each is authenticated by its relation to the other. Preaching in fact derives its substance from the sacrament which itself refers to an action in the total event of Revelation. Preaching is a commentary on and an interpretation of the sacrament, having the same meaning but in words. If this fact be recognized it will be clear that preaching is impossible except within the territory of the Church, in that setting where, in baptism and the Lord's Supper, man is chosen by God himself to belong to the body of Christ, to be nourished and protected during his journey to eternal life. And we should know that all those who hear are baptized and called to partake of grace, and what has been thus begun in them will be fulfilled.

In this way, by reference to baptism and the Lord's

Supper, the origin and the aim of preaching, and the course
it pursues, are more clearly defined and the place of the
messenger of the Word is more plainly seen.

Having discussed these theoretical questions let us consider what goes on in the evangelical Church. At the outset
something appears to be lacking. In those circles which
embraced the Reformation, the sacramental Church of
Rome was replaced by a Church of the Word. Very soon,
preaching became the centre of worship and the celebration
of the sacrament came to occupy a more restricted place,
so that today in the Roman Church, the Church of the
sacrament, preaching has little significance, while in the
Reformed Church the sacrament, while it exists, does not
form an integral and necessary element of worship. These
two positions are in effect a destruction of the Church.
What meaning can there be in preaching which exalts itself
at the expense of the sacrament, and does not look back to
the sacrament which it should interpret? Our life does not
depend on what the minister may be able to say, but on the
fact that we are baptized, that God has called us. This lack
has indeed been recognized, and attempts have been made
to fill it by various means (reform of the liturgy, beauti-
fying worship with music, etc.). But these palliative
measures are bound to fail because they do not touch the
real issue.

Those who advocate such methods of renewing the forms
of worship take their stand—mistakenly—on Luther. But
he, seeking to retain all that was of value in the Roman
liturgy, gave first place to the Lord's Supper. Calvin, also,
constantly emphasized the necessity for a service of Communion at every Sunday worship. And this is precisely
what we lack today: the sacrament every Sunday. The
order of worship should be as follows: at the beginning of
the service, public baptism; at the end, the Lord's Supper;
between the two sacraments, the sermon, which in this way
would be given its full significance. This would indeed be

preaching the pure Word and duly ministering the sacraments!

So long as the true significance of evangelical worship in its totality is not understood, no theological efforts or liturgical movements will be efficacious. Only when worship is rightly ordered, with preaching and sacrament, will the liturgy come into its own, for it is only in this way that it can fulfil its office, which is to lead to the sacrament. The administration of the sacraments must not be separated from the preaching of the Gospel, because the Church is a physical and historical organism, a real and visible body as well as the invisible, mystical body of Christ, and because she is both these at once.

There is no doubt that we should be better Protestants if we allowed ourselves to be instructed in this matter by Roman Catholicism; not to neglect preaching, as it so often does, but to restore the sacrament to its rightful place. It is open to question whether the motive for our liturgical efforts is anything more than a desire to approach nearer to the 'beautiful services' of the Church of Rome. But what is rightly to be sought is not an elaboration of the liturgy but the true significance of the sacrament in the Church. A good Protestant will allow himself to admit this, and at the same time will insist on good preaching.

In preaching all that is necessary is to recount again what concerns the prior event of Revelation. And in order to distinguish the two actions to which Revelation refers, the preacher may point to the sacrament on the one hand and Holy Scripture on the other; the one looks back to the act of Revelation which God accomplished: the other refers to the nature of the Revelation. It is idle to oppose sacrament to preaching; they cannot be separated since they are two aspects of the same thing.

The Divine act of revelation took place at the heart of human life and history. The Church, however, cannot hand it on directly. In Holy Scripture the truth and actuality of the Revelation are preserved, for Scripture represents the testimony of chosen intermediaries, the prophets and apostles. The Church rests on the foundation of witnesses individually called to be apostles. When witness is borne to the Revelation—that is to say, when Scripture is read and expounded—the Church should understand that she does not live for herself alone; her life is not her own nor does it rest on its own foundation; but the Church is founded on the sole and unique action of God accomplished in Israel and in Christ—those two centres of Revelation : a people and a Saviour. On the one hand that erring people who, through their inability to keep the Law, so frequently lapsed into sin, but were never abandoned by God; on the other, the overflowing of grace, the Saviour of the people, the fulfilment of the Law and, in consequence, the Gospel.

It is clear that Revelation is not to be thought of as a general principle, regulating the relations between God and the world. On the contrary, it is one unique event. Scripture, therefore, has a concrete quality and is not an intellectual system. The fact of holding closely to Scripture bears witness to the unique character—unique in time and in method—of Revelation.

In her relationship with God the Church represents not human kind in general, but men gathered together by the work of Revelation; for this reason she is based on the Scriptures. If, then, the Church is constituted by the testimony of the apostles, the mediators of Revelation, what, in this context, is the function of preaching? It is, simply, to make this witness understood.

This leads to a consideration of preaching from a text; the text will always be from the Bible and will relate at once to the sacrament and to the Word of the prophets and apostles. No reasons can be given for preferring the Bible nor is it necessary to justify the choice. The starting point is the fact that the Church is the place where the Bible is open; there God has spoken and still speaks. There we are given our mission and our orders. By taking our stand on the Bible we dare to do what has to be done. These writings which lie before us are prior to our testimony, and our preaching must take into account what has already been given. We can no more liberate ourselves from the Bible than a child can liberate himself from his father.

In conclusion it may be said that the ecclesiastical character of preaching is guaranteed so long as it is inspired by the sacrament and is faithful to Scripture.

3. *Preaching and Doctrine*

It has already been shown that preaching is subject to an order; it is a mission and a command, and therefore has a relation to doctrine.

In setting out to educate men, it is possible to follow a scheme and determine one's aim. This method could be applied by the preacher also if it were the Church's task to educate humanity and make human beings into real men. But if the true function of the Church be understood, it cannot proceed thus. The Church is not an institution intended to keep the world on the right path nor is it dedicated to the service of progress. It is not an ambulance on the battle-fields of life. On the other hand, it must not seek to establish an ideal community, whether of souls, hearts, or spirits. No doubt all these things have their value and should engage one's attention. They can, moreover, be accessories to preaching and can play a part in it, as they do in ordinary life. The preacher, like other Christians, lives in the world and cannot avoid these things. But the moment he makes them his chief object, the preacher ceases to have any justification for preaching.

This is becoming more and more obvious today when all the various civilizing agencies have been taken over by organizations other than the Church. If the Church were to disappear—a point of view expressed by Richard Rothe, for example, who advocated the progressive fusion of

Church and State—the press, the radio, social welfare
schemes, psychology, and politics would suffice to care for
the life of the family and of the soul. As regards public
morals and similar preoccupations, the children of this
world know more about them than the Church does and
have access to more efficient methods. In these circumstances the Church is merely the fifth wheel of the carriage
—and not even a spare wheel!

It is necessary, therefore, to consider seriously the
mission laid upon the Church. What is needed are men who
are obedient to an order given to them from outside themselves, to a necessity prior to everything which determines
our earthly existence, such as birth or death. The Church is
obliged to recognize precisely that an order has been given
which must be carried out. The Church can justify her existence only in so far as she understands that she is founded
on a call. Therefore she has no plan—for the plan is God's
—but only a task to fulfil. Preaching, set within the frame
of worship, should be the proclamation of the Church's
obedience to the task committed to her by Christ.

From all this the following considerations emerge :

1. Preaching must faithfully adhere to doctrine, that is,
to the Confession of our faith,[1] which is not a summary of
the religious ideas drawn from our own inner consciousness, but a statement of what we believe and confess
because we have received it and have heard the Word of
Revelation. The Confession is man's response to what God
has said and every sermon is a response for which the
preacher is responsible.

Preaching, therefore, has nothing to do with any scheme
or notion which the preacher has wrought out in his own
mind. Here only obedience is required; in other words,
having heard the Word of God he responds in accordance
with the Confession of faith. Naturally one is not required

[1] E.g., the Augsburg Confession (Lutheran), or the Westminster
Confession (Presbyterian).—Ed.

to preach confessions of faith, but to have as the purpose and limit of one's message the Confession of one's Church, taking one's stand where Church stands.

2. A second, practical consequence concerns the element of edification; what is to be built up? Clearly, the Church itself. But building up the Church is not to be understood in the sense given to it in *The Shepherd of Hermas*,[1] where it means 'to go on building', 'to build upon an edifice in course of construction'. To build up the Church means to rebuild each time from foundation to roof. The Church has to be re-making itself continually; continually the orders given have to be accepted, obedience has constantly to be learnt again. 'From obedience to obedience' is the journey of the Christian. The Church is a community placed under Revelation and built up by hearing the Word of God, built up by the grace of God in order that it may live. In this context then, but only there, can one speak of educating men, of giving moral and spiritual help to humanity; there is a place for such secondary structures in the shadow of the main building. 'Seek ye first the Kingdom of God and his righteousness'; 'one thing is needful.'

4. *The Example of the Apostles*

At the heart of the Church which is commissioned to proclaim the good news, an individual emerges from the midst of the community to bear witness before it to man's redemption and salvation in Christ. In connexion with the question of doctrinal fidelity already discussed, there arises the problem of the legitimacy of this individual action. Apart from the responsibility of the apostolate, there is no special emphasis in the New Testament on the function of the preacher. From the indications given concerning those appointed to this duty by the apostles and recognized as such by the community, no doctrine of the function of preaching can be elicited.

[1] This dates from the second century in Rome.—Ed.

The apostolic function is always linked with the foundation and the existence of the Church. In Matt. 16.18-19 (cf. Matt. 18.15-20) the Church is represented as established according to a specific order. Peter represents the apostles and the community is distinct from the apostolate.

In the period after the apostolic age, the Church is described as one and holy (*ecclesia una sancta*), one, that is, in so far as it is at once teaching (*ecclesia docens*) and listening (*ecclesia audiens*); and wherever the Church is, the same situation exists. The conditions of its origin are not repeated because the apostolate was constituted only once. But those men who, following in the footsteps of the apostles, are called to that mission, must continue to do as the apostles did. In so far as the Church is the Body of Christ, the preacher is, in a sense, successor of the apostles and vicar of Christ. The preaching and the Church are one, for 'there can be no Word of God apart from the people of God' (Luther).

Following the apostles, the preacher, as a minister of lower rank, does in one particular community what the apostles did for the whole Church. When God himself invests a man with the office of 'vicar of Christ', the question of the particular individual who receives this charge is of secondary importance. What is important is to be sure that the Church is indeed the Church of Jesus Christ; that when someone speaks the Word and others hear it, it is indeed the Word of God that is heard and received by the action of the Holy Spirit. Luther said: 'Wherever this Gospel is sincerely preached, there is the Kingdom of Christ. Wherever the Word is, there is the Holy Spirit, whether in the hearer or in the teacher.'

All those marks of an authentic ministry which can be listed are relative because they can only be human criteria. Nevertheless four of these criteria may be retained, because on them may be said to depend, from the human point of view, the legitimacy of the preacher's function.

1. The preacher must be conscious of an interior call. He must experience the imperative pressure of a vocation and accept it with all his heart. But this 'I cannot do otherwise' raises all kinds of questions. For example, the alleged interior necessity could perhaps be the satisfaction of a personal desire. It may be noted that the interior call which we think we recognize is not decisive unless it derives not from our knowledge or feeling but from that commanding voice which is God's.

2. The passages in the Pastoral Epistles (I Tim. 3.1-7, 8-13; II Tim. 4.1, 5-9) concerning bishops and deacons contain lists of Greek-sounding virtues and rules relating to the man who assumes the function of a preacher. 'He must be above reproach', he must not compromise his function by a way of life which runs counter to contemporary morals and customs. He must not, by any eccentricity of behaviour, draw attention to himself and thereby divert it from the Gospel. These ethical precepts are evidently intended as a reminder that the minister of the Word is responsible before God. But if it is recognized that these orders proceed from the Law of God the preacher must realize that he is constantly at fault. He is able to stand before God only because he is justified in Christ by faith.

3. On the other hand, in the Pastoral Epistles again, the preacher is required to be skilled (I Tim. 3.2; II Tim. 2.24). The Church has been accustomed to understand by this a systematic training in theology. The preacher has no right to rely on the Holy Spirit in matters for which he is responsible, without making any effort himself. With all modesty and earnestness he must labour and strive to present the Word aright, even though he is fully aware that only the Holy Spirit can in fact 'teach aright'. The Church, therefore, if it is conscious of its responsibilities, cannot admit that anyone, whoever he may be, has the right to preach the Word without theological training. Nevertheless, it should not be forgotten that true preaching is learnt

from the Holy Spirit, theological training being sub-
ordinated to him.

4. It has already been pointed out that the office of the
preacher is different from that of the apostles; he is placed
in the position he holds by the will of the community. The
function he exercises belongs to the Church; it derives from
the community and is exercised within it. But the fact of
being appointed by the community does not make it less
necessary for him to have been called to this duty by God.

We have already noted four characteristic marks of God's
calling, but it is not for us to fix the limits of that call.
God has founded the Church, and has instituted the
ministry; he chooses the man who is to exercise it, acting
in this matter where and how he wills. Nevertheless, such a
man must always answer to the four qualifications which
are the marks of God's calling, which itself remains the
ultimate question for him. The divine call gives to these
human criteria whatever weight they have, while at the
same time emphasizing their merely relative character. On
this point there can be no dispute; we can only hear the call
and give effect to it by going forward, accepting the
ministry with all the demands which it entails. Thus,
through our obedience, the Revelation and the Church,
whose responsibility it is to preach the Word, are made
visible.

When the preacher regards his ministry in this light, he
will not seek the satisfaction of his own interests or in-
clinations, of his own convictions or his own desires. But
even if considerations of this sort do enter in, one reality
must be apparent in his every action : God has spoken and
he speaks. Wherever human will and action are brought
into subjection to the will and action of God, there legitimate Christian preaching is found.

How is the preacher to be faithful to the example of the
apostles? The hearer earnestly hopes to learn something of
the great work to which the preacher to whom he listens is

dedicated, though he is only a man limited by his human nature and condition. But the activity in which he engages is problematical and even, in a sense, impossible. It is a fact, however, that it has pleased God to intervene on the human plane by means of a man, in spite of the inherent weaknesses of human nature. The preacher who strives to be faithful to the example of the apostles is aware of the inevitable imperfections in what he does, but he will not allow himself to be paralysed by his weakness; he finds his strength in the reality of God's revelation of himself. He knows that the divine will, which has made itself known and which is active on the human level, will clothe his feebleness and his wretchedness and will endue his action with a quality which he himself cannot give it.

Drawing life from God's forgiveness, he will carry out his task simply in obedience, without letting himself be intimidated, because he knows that God has commanded it.

It is important to note that this faithfulness to the apostolic example cannot be characterized by any single psychological quality either in the preacher or his hearers. Simplicity or objectivity may give a clue; or perhaps effectiveness, for example, an awakening in the community. But such things cannot be regarded as valid criteria. The only thing that counts is to make the Word of God heard. And it is not possible to know what happens at that point, because the effect produced by the Word depends on God. So we leave it in his hands, trusting in him and in what he has done.

It was pointed out above that the Church needs to be constantly renewed; it is always being created by the preaching and hearing of the Word. Thus the organized Church is the expectant Church; it is moving along the road where the event which creates the Church takes place.

The same point of view applies to the man who is singled out from the rest of the community in order to exercise in it a particular ministry. This act is efficacious by virtue of the vocation bestowed by God. Ordination, therefore, is not an act of ecclesiastical jurisdiction, but a recognition of the divine call. Naturally, the man who is ordained must receive the Word of God which is expressed in ordination, a Word which he must constantly receive afresh in his ministry.

The appointment of a man to the ministry is a question, not of theology, but of ecclesiastical practice. It is obvious that behind this calling, in the narrower sense, there must always be the total vocation of God.

Thus, as regards the government and order of the Church, the four criteria which we have discussed must be taken into account. The Church cannot allow anyone to arrogate to himself a function unless he meets the requirements of these criteria. At the same time, in addition to the 'ordinary' vocation there may always be the possibility of a vocation which is 'extraordinary'. God is not limited by the Church's ordinance; he may be pleased to call a man from outside the ecclesiastical organization to preach his Word. But the vocation of such a man will have to be examined and tested by the Church in relation to its faithfulness to Scripture.

In considering the constituent elements of preaching it will be well to define a term already used above. Mention has been made of 'an attempt' which the Church has been commanded to make. The question suggested by the word 'attempt' invites consideration of the provisional nature of preaching.

5. *The Provisional Character of Preaching*

The word 'provisional' (*vorläufig*) is used here in a wider sense than it ordinarily has. It signifies also 'that which has not yet attained its end'. By preaching's 'provisional' or 'antecedent' character should be understood the fact that it precedes something of which it is the harbinger, as the herald (*Vorläufer*) precedes (*vorauslaufen*) a king.

Here we approach the point where justification leads to

sanctification. Preaching is a human activity and thus stained with sin, but it is also both commanded and blest by God and therefore a promise is attached to it. The following sections will deal with preaching in relation to ethics and the law and will involve the dogmatic concepts of justification and sanctification.

If preaching is considered as a human activity, immediately man's incapacity and unworthiness in relation to God are clearly seen. And yet this activity is of the greatest import—not indeed in itself, because the fact that the preacher has performed his task does not confer on him any sort of title. His title derives from the concepts of Revelation, the Church, faithfulness in doctrine, faithfulness to the apostolic example, discussed above. This means that the preacher, precisely because he, a sinner, has performed his task, is driven back to Christ, the Lord of the Church, by whom he is justified. He, most of all, is confronted by the necessity of living by that divine action which justifies him, by the faith which is summed up in the words: 'Fear not, only believe.'

Nevertheless, it is not to be supposed that thereby a transformation is effected in him; or that he is infused with a new nature deriving from a superior being and enriching him. By no means: justification is the light of God's countenance shed on a man who still remains a man. In this context, new life means contemplating that light and living by it. Salvation, in the eschatological sense, abolishes the opposition between the old and the new; salvation is to be understood as the fulfilment, in the future, of what we now have and are by the promise. Preaching is an attempt undertaken with human means, which are, in all respects, inadequate. Here a man cannot rely on his own resources. But, in the eyes of God, who raises the dead and brings to life that which is not, this attempt is a 'good work' to which his promise and his blessing are attached. But only in so far as it is in fact undertaken by his command.

Another aspect of the question presents itself : how can a man's action be good and holy? What is the situation of a sinner who, having been forgiven, is called to preach the Word? There is no question here of virtue, but only of obedience in face of the goodness of God. The basis of preaching—a human action sanctified by God—is a demand made by God. The preacher has a part in the new life because God wills to take him to himself, he claims him for himself. Anyone who attempts to set limits of any kind to that demand clearly has not understood what has happened; a man has been summoned by God, he has been taken prisoner, he hears his Word. This is the sanctification of the messenger of Jesus Christ.

The preacher, like every Christian indeed, is not an isolated individual. Even though, after his call, he is the same man that he was before, he is set in an entirely new situation. Nothing that we can say about the revivifying power of the Word of God can adequately describe the perturbation and the peace which possess a man who has been laid hold of by the call of Jesus Christ. When God thus turns towards man, all things inevitably become new!

But then a man's mind turns to his own conduct and way of life. What will this new thing, this new life become in his own life? At all events his life is no longer at the mercy of chance; he is no longer in command, no longer his own master; he is the servant of a Lord. He no longer goes through life heedlessly exposed to all kinds of danger; he is called to walk in obedience to the commands of his Lord.

This emphasis on its provisional nature brings us to the central problem of all preaching. The Church is the hand-maid of Christ on earth. Our situation is described in a passage of the Bible which is of particular importance for the preacher—Psalm 119. In its 176 verses one theme is discussed in all its aspects : a man is summoned, is justified, and rejoices because there is a commandment, a law, and a way.

This 'provisional character' becomes precisely the field of battle and of labour. How is it to be done? An answer to this question will now be attempted.

6. Preaching and the Scriptures

The purpose of preaching is to explain the Scriptures. What ought to be set forth in this human discourse? Since the only reason for preaching is to show God's work of justification, the preacher is not required to develop a system of his own, to enlarge on what he thinks about his own life and that of his neighbour, his reflections on society or the world. If he lives by justification he cannot take account of human ideologies. Men do not live by the intrinsic values of things. If we ask what we are justified by, we are always recalled to the four keynotes of Holy Scripture, which bears witness to Revelation, establishes the Church, hands on the mission (the power to bear witness) and creates vocations. There is, therefore, nothing to be said which is not already to be found in the Scriptures. No doubt the preacher will be conscious of the weight of his own ideas which he drags after him; but ultimately he must decide whether he will allow himself to compromise or whether, in spite of all the notions at the back of his mind, he will accept the necessity of expounding the Book and nothing else.

In order to avoid being submerged in general considerations, we shall discuss, under five heads, the behaviour and the qualities proper to a Christian preacher.

1. First, quite simply, *to put his trust in Scripture*. All that is required of a preacher is to keep to the text and confine his discourse to expounding it. If he feels that the Bible does not provide everything necessary for living and that he must add some practical instruction, then his trust is not complete.

2. *To explain Scripture* means to respect it, in the sense of the Latin *respicere* (to have regard for something to

which one looks for help). All discourse must issue from such respect. The preacher is concerned with something other than himself, and he has no thought for anything besides. He may be compared to a man who is reading something with great difficulty and is astonished by the discoveries he makes; his lips move, he spells out rather than reads, he is all eyes, he is possessed by a deep conviction : 'this is not the work of men.'

3. *Close and detailed attention to the text* is indispensable. Perhaps 'zeal' rather than 'attention' would better describe the effort of concentration which he must apply to getting at the meaning of the passage he is studying. This will require scientific exegetical methods, involving accurate historical and linguistic study, for the Bible is a historical document which came into being in the context of human society.

From beginning to end the Bible is concerned with one unique theme which is, however, presented in many different ways. As a result of this variety each passage, at every period of time, speaks to man's needs. Thus, not only is linguistic study needed, but it is also necessary to search in the Scriptures for God's message for society.

No preaching is acceptable if this preparatory work has obviously not been thoroughly done. Moreover, a respectful regard for the text, constantly renewed, is also necessary. This is where the minister who is absorbed in practical activities has to struggle against intellectual laziness. In the pulpit on Sunday this negligence becomes apparent, for at that moment all the zeal that he may display cannot make up for indolence. In this connexion, the congregation ought to allow the preacher more leisure to prepare his discourse, for adequate preparation demands plenty of time. On the other hand, the Church should see to it that only properly prepared sermons are delivered from the pulpit.

4. *The duty of avoiding pretentiousness.* The Scriptures provide the answer to man's questions, and he should be

content with that. There is no need for him to put himself forward by displaying his own aptitudes, however good. If the preacher is attentive he will always find an answer in the Scriptures; he is driven to the limits of his own thinking, he is brought face to face with the prophets and apostles. Then he, and his own views and spiritual insight, must retreat.

However alert his mind, man always tends to tread in the well-worn paths. For this reason, even after the most fruitful study and in spite of all the efforts of imagination, one still does not know what one has to say; one is at most prepared for the situation in which the Word of God has to be spoken. In fact, in that situation, a man is already filled, although he has not yet realized it. It is possible to speak, for example, of the exalted morality, the power of the language and thought of the Bible, and many other topics. But this is not the Gospel, for the Gospel is not to be found in our thoughts or in our hearts, but in the Scriptures. The most cherished habits, the purest intentions must all be renounced in order that one may be able to hear; nothing must be allowed to stifle those living things which spring from the Bible. Again and again one must submit to being thwarted, must yield oneself to be made use of, must abandon everything which stands in the way.

The danger of pretentiousness is a reason for exercising some caution in regard to the sermons of Luther, for example. Modesty was not always his strong point. After his great discovery he felt impelled to dwell on the unique idea which inspired him. He neglected whole pages in the Bible—for example, those concerned with the Law and rewards—because he was in a sense bewitched by the revelation of justification by faith.

Ideas which occupy the mind must be subject to correction by the text of Scripture; one must not adopt the demeanour of one who knows in advance what the truth is. What sort of modesty is that?

5. *The preacher must yield himself to the movement of the Word of God.* It is easy to say, or to have read somewhere, that the Bible is the Word of God without knowing what this really means. It is in fact not true in the sense that the Civil Code embodies the thought of the State. A more precise statement of the truth would be to say that the Bible *becomes* God's Word, and when it becomes this for us, then it is so.

The preacher is called to share an experience with the Bible; a perpetual exchange takes place between himself and the Word of God; the preacher must be submissive to the movement of that Word, allowing himself to be led through the Scriptures.

The 'Canon of Scripture' is indeed a guarantee, but it means merely that the Church takes these writings to be the place where the Word of God is to be heard. Finally, as regards the 'doctrine of inspiration', it is not enough to believe in it; one must ask oneself: am I expecting it? Will God speak to me in this Scripture? This expectation must be active; it means giving oneself to the Scriptures, seeking in order that one may be found.

The five points which have been considered, and which characterize the biblical quality of preaching, do not represent simply a theological point of view which may or may not be taken account of. Rather they describe a discipline to be submitted to. It is not possible to avoid it without at the same time relinquishing one's profession.

It remains to draw attention to three very serious consequences which may result from neglecting the requirements described above.

(a) The preacher should never be so puffed up by the consciousness of his mission and his function or his theology, as to feel himself inspired by the Holy Spirit to represent God's interests to the world. There is no antidote to this disease except the strength which springs from a true understanding of Scripture. Where Holy Scripture reigns supreme no seed of sacerdotalism can grow. But the preacher can never rest in a false security or cherish self-satisfaction.

(b) The preacher must not be a visionary, soaring into an unreal world, though his mind may be, no doubt, full of good intentions and noble ideas. Faithful preaching is not visionary, for Holy Scripture was shaped in a very real world. He may, at times, feel himself to be a solitary, but he should never let himself be carried away by dreams and raptures.

(c) The preacher must not be tedious. For long enough the words 'minister' and 'boredom' have been regarded as practically synonymous. Congregations often believe that they have known for years everything which is said from the pulpit, and this is not entirely their fault. Here again, the remedy is to preach the authentic truth of Scripture. If preaching is faithful to the Bible it cannot be tedious. Scripture is in fact so interesting, it has so many new and startling things to tell us, that those who listen cannot possibly be overcome with sleep.

There is still a question which requires an answer : how should the preacher deal with the Old Testament? The Old Testament mainly concerns us through its relation to the New Testament. If the Church is represented as the successor of the synagogue, then the Old Testament witnesses to Christ before Christ (but not apart from Christ). The Old and New Testaments are related to one another as prophecy to its fulfilment, and the Old Testament should always be regarded in this light.

Historical exegesis should not be neglected, but it is always necessary to consider whether an interpretation based on the historical situation takes account of the unity of the two Testaments. Even in a sermon on Judges 6.36, for example, it will be possible to adhere to the literal meaning of the text, and at the same time to point towards Jesus

Christ. The Old Testament, though a completely Jewish
book, none the less refers to Christ.

In considering how far the use of allegory is legitimate,
the relation between the Old and New Testaments provides
guidance. In order to avoid the temptation to give to a
passage a meaning which is not there, it is wise to keep to
what is actually said in that passage, while bearing in mind
that the Church adopted the Old Testament because of
Christ. At the same time historical and Christian interpre-
tations should not be opposed to one another. The Old
Testament looks forward, and the New Testament speaks of
the future while looking back, and both look to Christ.

7. *Originality in Preaching*

At the beginning of this study, among certain basic
definitions, it was stated that a man is concerned 'to proclaim to his fellow men what God himself has to say to
them by explaining, in his own words, a passage from
Scripture which concerns them personally'. The phrase 'in
his own words' leads to a consideration of what may be
called originality in preaching. The preacher, a sinful
creature, is called to expound a text faithfully; but fidelity
to his text is not a screen behind which he disappears. His
words do not express ready-made ideas which he has
swallowed whole—somewhat in the manner of the 'infused
grace' of some theologians. The man who speaks is a real
man of flesh and blood, with a personality and a history
and a background of his own, whom God has laid hold of
in the actual situation in which he is placed.

The minister must not pose as a Luther or a Calvin or
a prophet; when he is explaining his text let him be simply
himself. His sermon is the message of a man of his own time
and he is responsible for it. One who has heard the Word
is called upon to repeat what he has heard, and it is important that he should be himself, as he is, especially when
he bears an apostolic responsibility. It is not fitting that he

should act a part, dress up his ideas in a spectacular fashion, deck his discourse with ornaments. A mission is entrusted to him, not as minister or theologian nor as a man who enjoys special privileges, but as a servant. He should then fulfil his task simply and naturally.

In this connexion, however, a warning is called for; the word 'originality' has dubious and even dangerous associations. It does not apply to one who imagines himself to possess, by virtue of some sort of religious experience, a certain independence in relation to God. It can be applied to a man who lives continually in the consciousness that his sins are forgiven. It does not refer to a so-called 'existential attitude', for this fantasy of existentialism is simply the old Satan, who has disguised himself under a new mask to deceive humanity.

The following practical directions bear on the subject of this chapter.

(a) The preacher, having thoroughly prepared himself, comes before his congregation, first and foremost, as a man who has been pierced by the Word of God and has been led to repentance in the face of divine judgment; but also as a man who has received with thankfulness the Gospel of forgiveness and is able to rejoice in it. Only in this progression through judgment and grace can preaching become genuinely original.

(b) Then he must have the courage to tell others what this experience means to him; the testimony he offers to his hearers will be the fruit of his own study and meditation. He is called on to speak of what he lives by and this he will do within an authentic biblical setting, but not in the form of an exegetical discourse. His very first sentence must be a challenge addressed to the individual hearer, but also an integral part of his text.

(c) His preaching must be personal. A preacher may, perhaps, draw his inspiration from a model, but once in the pulpit he should be simply himself. He is the one who has been called, he it is who must speak; the finest thoughts, once they have been borrowed and transformed on the lips of another, are no longer what they were. Let there be no posturing in borrowed plumes!

(d) Let him speak in the way that is natural to him, rather than assuming in the pulpit the cloak of an alien speech. Even the language of the Bible or of poetry, as also the ringing tones of an impressive peroration, are unsuited to the task he has in hand.

(e) Let him be simple. Those who are engaged in this enterprise should follow the path on which the Bible leads them, should see things as they are and as they unfold in actual experience. This will preserve them from displays of doctrinal erudition which are of no great importance. Christian truth is always new when it is set in the context of daily life.

8. *Adapting Preaching to the Congregation*

A preacher is called to lead to God the people whom he sees before him; God desires him to preach to these people here present. But he must approach them as people who are already the objects of God's action, for whom Christ died and has risen again. He has to tell them, therefore, that God's mercy avails for them as truly today as at the beginning of time. That is what is meant by adapting preaching to the congregation, from which it follows that:

1. The preacher will love his congregation and feel that he is one with them; his constant thought will be: 'These are my people and I long to share with them what God has given to me.' To speak in the most eloquent language, even with the tongues of angels, will avail nothing if love is lacking.

2. Because he loves it, the preacher will live the life of his congregation, placing himself on their level. He does not have to be the wise man of the people, the village diviner who lays bare the innermost thoughts of men's

hearts, but the question of what their thoughts really are is always in his mind.

3. Preaching is not intended to be simply a clearer and more adequate explanation of life than can be arrived at by other means. Certainly this aspect must be taken into account, but it should be kept in the background. The congregation is waiting for the meaning of life to be illumined by the light of God, and not to be offered high-sounding speeches.

No doubt the preacher will give heed to all these things, and no one will surpass him in heartfelt sympathy, but the faithfulness of his preaching will most clearly be seen in the way he lives.

4. Tact—knowing what it is permissible to say to each individual—is indispensable. Frequently it seems that something ought to be said, and that the Bible provides justification for doing so, whereas, in fact, the motive is pride. Then good relations become needlessly embittered.

In this connexion, it may be pointed out again that, in a sermon, biblical criticism should take a subordinate place and be exercised only in a humble and reverent spirit; there is no need to make an idol of truth.

5. Here Tillich's phrase 'awareness of the present moment' is important, if given its right place. What demands does the contemporary situation make on the preacher and his congregation? Together they are sharing an historical experience; the words of the preacher must be relevant to the immediate preoccupations of his hearers. If this were understood, preachers would be on their guard against continuing to discourse on topics which have long ceased to be important.

These notes on how to adapt one's preaching to one's congregation should suffice to show that preaching is not a service performed for clients. Neither is the preacher a dictator, nor an orator, nor yet a hermit dwelling apart from his congregation.

D

9. *The Inspiration of Preaching*

Preaching is 'God's own Word', that is to say, through the activity of preaching, God himself speaks. If it were not so, the preacher who acted on what has been said so far, would have laboured in vain and would be but an unprofitable servant. This ministry of the Word depends entirely on what God wills to make of it. Therefore it follows that the preacher must be clothed with humility; that, because of his function as a human mouthpiece, he will be discreet and sober; that, since preaching is, by definition, concerned solely with God, it is not possible to preach without praying that the words spoken may become the call of God to men; and, moreover, the whole congregation should join in this prayer.

The present discussion has now reached the limit of what human speech can express, the point where the Holy Spirit himself must intercede for us 'with groanings that cannot be uttered'.

VI

PREPARING A SERMON

SOMETIMES A minister, when preparing his sermon, feels impelled to say everything he has in the depths of his heart; at other times he may feel embarrassed because he is not very sure what special message he has to give. Neither of these situations need be taken too seriously; he ought to know that what he has to say will be given to him. He should therefore try to control, to some extent, what comes into his mind and to listen, or rather allow himself to be comforted by Him who gives what he demands. Are there not also the Old and New Testaments which still have something to say?

1. *The Choice of a Text*

The preacher, then, has the Scriptures before him, and two things have to be considered: what has to be done and what he has no right to do. Whenever one chooses a text a decision has to be made: whether to obey or to disobey the Word, that is, God himself. Disobedience consists in imagining that it is possible to approach Scripture with full freedom to exercise one's own unfettered powers. If, on the other hand, one puts oneself at God's disposal, that obedience will guide one's choice.

There can be no thought of arbitrarily laying hold of Scripture in order to find in it a text which will suit oneself, which seems appropriate to what one wishes to say. The sacred text is not to be treated according to our own desires; it must be in command; it is above us and we are its servants. In order to avoid going astray in this way, the following points should be kept in mind:

1. Do not choose too short a text, for the danger just described will be greater than if a whole section of a book is being dealt with. For example, it is not advisable to detach from their contexts the first Beatitude or I John 4.16; such texts may tempt the preacher to use them as material on which to exercise his own eloquence. If preaching is essentially exposition of the Bible, it will be well to avoid short texts.

2. Beware of passages which are considered easy and are frequently quoted. Thus, when commemorating the Reformation, do not arbitrarily distort the meaning of Gal. 5.1; on All Souls' Day, do not give to John 11.3 and 16 a different significance from that which the context requires. The illuminating power of a biblical phrase is always greater in the context in which God has placed it than in discourses, however beautiful and arresting, which do violence to the Word of God.

3. Do not indulge in allegory; exercising one's talents on the Word hinders it from sounding out clearly. One should also beware of intruding one's own individuality or enlarging on one's personal experience by using illustrations or parables drawn from events in one's own life.

4. Preaching should not be directed to a utilitarian purpose; do not use Psalm 96 to encourage better singing or as a eulogy of music!

5. In order that the same passages of Scripture should not recur too frequently in his sermons, a preacher would do well to keep to a plan based on the Church's year, or deliver a course of sermons on one book. It may happen, as a result of his repeated contacts with the Scriptures, that certain passages impress the preacher with the force of a command. It goes without saying that a minister consults his Bible on other occasions as well as when he is preparing a sermon.

6. It is not possible, in one sermon, to discourse on a particular subject (thematic preaching) and to expound a

passage of Scripture (homiletic). Within the Church the preacher is not required to discuss Christian principles or similar topics; what needs to be heard is what God has to say to the Church, which constitutes its foundation and its building up. If an evangelistic mission is planned in order to draw into the Church those who are still outside, we should not begin by evading the special service which has been laid upon us.

7. Avoid drawing special attention to particular events or commemorations. Anything which the congregation could profitably take note of will find an echo in the sermon; otherwise the matter can be passed over in silence. But the decision does not rest with the preacher; it will depend on what the Word of God requires of him. The Scriptures must occupy a clearly defined place in the preacher's mind and to ensure this he must submit himself to a rigorous discipline; he must be attentive only to the Word, not to what the public or the congregation or his own heart desires to hear.

2. *The Receptive Attitude*

The term 'receptive' is the opposite of 'spontaneous'. In other words, it signifies being passive, or being acted on as object, as opposed to being active, or acting as subject (these last two terms, should, however, always be used with caution). The point is to hear what the text has to say. One may begin quite simply by reading it and pondering it word by word; here lies the content of the sermon. But the text must be read in the original, for any translation is a secondary source and, in fact, a commentary.

At the outset, therefore, we are confronted with the important question of language. It is not suggested that Hebrew and Greek possess some special quality which made them fit to be used by the Holy Spirit as the vehicle of the Word of God. Nevertheless Revelation is conveyed in these languages and it is necessary therefore to work with these documents. From listening to a sermon it is possible to tell whether or not the preacher has used the original text, for in the original certain relations and connexions are to be found which are not apparent in a translation.

After this, different versions may be consulted. The preacher should not read his own translation to the congregation, but in the course of his sermon he might well draw attention to corrections and shades of meaning.

After a careful reading of the passage, the question of its content has to be considered. First the context in which it occurs must be given its full weight, for no Biblical passage is an isolated and detached piece of writing; it is set in a specific context, it is part of a whole. Many sermons would have quite a different bearing if what precedes and follows the particular passage had been duly taken into account.

Next comes the business of analysis. Certain points are to be noticed: the intention of the passage, its separate parts, the order in which the ideas occur; also the direction of its development; only at this point should commentaries be consulted. A commentary differs from a translation in that the several sections of the passage are subjected to detailed study. There are, generally speaking, two types of commentary: those dating from the end of the eighteenth century to the present day and those going back to an earlier date.

The former are characterized by their use of the results of historico-critical research, and these ought to be read. Historical criticism has led to a better understanding of the Scriptures than was possible in the past, for those situations which show the historical and secular aspects of the Bible have also something to teach us. Naturally this method raises certain problems which did not trouble the earlier commentators. However, in course of time historical criticism has assumed exaggerated importance, so that there is a tendency to identify the real meaning of Scripture with its historical significance. This attitude has in fact become a dogma, mainly held outside the Church, according to which man is the only maker of his world and of everything in it, including religion. Obviously, such a dogma provides no basis for a sermon. If it were valid the canonical rule binding us to the Bible would have no meaning, for outside the Bible there is a vast literature on this aspect of existence. But Holy Scripture is the only witness to God's revelation, the unique channel for the communication of the Word of God.

Nevertheless it is necessary to take account of those commentaries which derive from historical research. The fact that, in recent times, attention has been focused more particularly on the human side of the Bible, is no reason for ignoring that aspect; it should be remembered that Revelation is the Word made flesh and, by that token, it has become an event in history.

But then, how far does the human speech represent the Word of God? To what extent do the words of the Bible lead us, beyond their human authors, to 'Emmanuel'? No critical problem can absolve the student from asking himself this question and considering it seriously. The Word was indeed made flesh, but it is still the Word: this is the christological dogma of the Bible. The Bible represents men as constrained and subjugated by a truth which has laid hold of them; they speak of the Revelation they have received, and turn their eyes towards the Revelation which is to come. This is something which modern commentaries do not and cannot explain. Recourse must then be had to the earlier commentators (to whom the moderns often show themselves inferior in many ways), to the exegetical studies of Calvin and Luther and—with some reserve on account of Platonic influence—to those of Saint Augustine. Certain collections of sermons also, those of Calvin for example, are excellent expositions of Scripture.

Finally, some practical points may be mentioned. If, in exceptional circumstances, there is not sufficient time for such thorough preparation, the preacher should at least study the text in the original and in a good version; but this will certainly be a very rare occurrence. For those who —unlike the Church of Rome—possess this treasure—the Word—the preparation of his sermon will be the minister's prime duty.

If a discourse tends towards a too personal interpretation, the use of a commentary becomes absolutely necessary. Salutary warnings against a similar error are to be found in Scripture itself.

What should be the preacher's attitude towards a doubtful text? In the Church he is called to hear the Word of God; the verdict of the historian, therefore, does not in itself forbid the use of a text.

3. *The Direction of the Text*

When all the preliminary work already described has been done, the Bible is seen to be at once an historical book and the book of the Church. As an historical book it is a monument (*monumentum*—that which recalls the past) revealing something of the history of man's religious experience. This is, in fact, the aspect which modern commentators have thrown into relief. But there is much more in this book. For the preacher—as for everyone who reads the Bible as it ought to be read—it is, besides a monument referring to the past, a document which has a meaning for the present day. It tells of a decisive action performed once for all in the past but still relevant to us in our times; that is why the Bible is read today.

The Bible is the only record of Revelation, but the record is sufficient, and for this reason it is called Holy Scripture, the Word of God given to men. If it is recognized that this book is indeed the testimony of the Word of God, it may seem otiose to discuss subjects and theses in connexion with preaching; there can be no subject or thesis other than the Revelation of God, Jesus Christ.

It should, however, be remembered that what is presented in the biblical writings is not the Revelation itself but the witness to the Revelation, and this is expressed in human terms; it is given by prophets and apostles who spoke, not on their own authority but because they were constrained to do so (as Paul says), because they could not do otherwise (as the prophets say). They uttered their testimony as well as they could, conscious of their responsibility to the men to whom they spoke. The nature of the testimony is clearly shown in John 1.7-8. John the Baptist is not that light but he bears witness to it: 'Behold the Lamb of God who takes away the sin of the world.'

The preacher's task is to cause the testimony presented in the text to be heard; his preaching is good if it brings to life in this present age the testimony of the prophets and apostles. He is not required to discourse about well-known truths such as the excellence of faith, God and one's country or other subjects of that sort; he is required to recall that divine truth, constantly despised by men, and to do so with hope and prayer. In preaching he must always have in mind the thought that the truth which lies behind the words of the Bible is unknown to men; but that truth wills to be manifested, it must absolutely be known. But the preacher must not torture himself; he only has to strive, as the prophets and apostles strove, to say as best he may what they heard.

Three observations must be made on following the direction of the text:

1. It has been pointed out that the Bible is both a monument and a document. The document may have to be reconstituted, but it is not always necessary to restore the monument. Purely historical material is relevant only in so far as it forms part of the testimony. In preaching it is necessary to follow the direction of the text and to relate it to our own times; the text shows where the road leads, but we have to walk on it at the present day.

2. The preacher should be on his guard against always falling back on the same sort of plan, for instance, repeating in every sermon; 'Man is a sinner but Christ intervenes; man must mend his ways.' Scripture abounds in riches and offers an infinite variety of approaches. Bear this in mind and there will be something new to say every Sunday; and this will be a sign of the new beginning which we are undertaking with God, since he has been pleased to begin with us.

3. It is necessary once again to issue a warning against an arbitrary and too individual interpretation of Scripture. The best means of avoiding this is to keep constantly and closely in touch with the dogmatic teaching of the Church. Dogmas are like beacons and signposts marking the right direction. It is not the preacher's task to offer an exposition of dogmas and display his theological knowledge, but rather to use them as his guides.

4. *The Application of the Text*

Having considered the direction followed by the witness of the biblical authors, let us now turn our attention to the way in which this path may be trodden in our day, in the situation in which the congregation is now placed. These are the people to whom the preacher's words must be addressed and who need continually to hear the Word afresh. They are baptized into the Church and an appeal must be made to the faith which is grounded in baptism. Those to whom the preacher speaks have this in common : nothing is more certain than the fact they they will die.

But in order that the preacher may speak to them in a way that they will understand, he must know them as individuals; he must be acquainted with the conditions which shape their lives, with their capacities, and their potentialities for good and evil. Only so will he find the means to touch their hearts so that the Word may have significance for *them*.

It is useless to worry oneself about the question of how

a man can ever speak to another in such a way that his words evoke faith in the hearer. One should, rather, make every effort to ensure that one's sermon is not simply a monologue, magnificent perhaps, but not necessarily helpful to the congregation. Those to whom he is going to speak must constantly be present in the mind of the preacher while he is preparing his sermon. What he knows about them will suggest unexpected ideas and associations which will be with him as he studies his text and will provide the element of actuality, the application of his text to the contemporary situation. The results of his theological studies provide a solid foundation; the element of actuality will enable him to construct a Christian discourse.

In order to make this somewhat clearer, let us consider the following proposition: in preaching, explanation is related to application as subject to predicate. The direction or guiding principle of a sermon is determined by and in the Church as it is at this present moment. It is addressed, therefore, not to humanity in the abstract but to the living, breathing man of today, whether within the Church or still outside it. In speaking of the man of today who is there to hear the Word, the preacher as well as the hearer is included. Thus preaching cannot be a monologue which a speaker delivers concerning himself and his own sin, for then it would no longer be possible to speak of the Church as the Communion of Saints.

There is, however, another danger which perhaps is more to be feared because it is easier to fall into: the preacher may address the congregation from a standpoint outside it instead of making himself one with it. He ought to know what his real position is; undoubtedly he has a special function, but that function is entrusted to the Church, not to him personally. He has no right to regard himself as set on high because of his knowledge of theology, so that he may stoop down to the level of his poor people. He must realize that he himself continually needs to hear the Word

afresh. The recognition of this situation is the necessary
condition for achieving a sound application which will also
be an explanation.

When, in preparing a sermon, an effort is made to follow
faithfully the direction of the text, a serious difficulty
presents itself in regard to the application : how to be faithful to the text and also true to life in this present age. Woe
to the minister who does not see that the Word has a real
significance for the men of today! But that man is even
more to blame who recognizes what the Bible has to say to
modern man, but is afraid of causing scandal and thereby
betrays his calling.

The Word confronts modern man, to disturb and attack
him in order to lead him into the peace of God. This Word
must never be distorted or obstructed by laziness or disobedience. The preacher, therefore, must have the courage
to preach as he ought, courage that does not flinch from a
direct attack and is unmoved by the consequences which
may result from his obedience. If this courage is his, the
Word of the whole of Scripture will bear the responsibility.

To keep close to life and remain close to the text—this
difficulty, for which there is no solution, should be a warning to all. In thematic preaching, where it is so easy to
make a casual idea the centre of one's discourse, the
preacher is specially prone to do violence to the text in
attempting to get closer to actual life. It is only too easy to
mistake those beautiful thoughts so dear to our self-esteem
for the thoughts of the text, which are generally much less
comfortable and less suited to the fashion of the day. It is,
therefore, necessary to test most thoroughly the ideas about
the contemporary situation which crowd into our minds,
and to sift them by reference to our text. This may force us
to discard some of our finest thoughts because the tenor
of the text demands it. There is no need to be distressed
because a sermon may have to go forward with some
broken limbs; it will not necessarily be slipshod or in-

adequate. This is where real courage is displayed before men and, at the same time, humility before the Word—that true humility which is fitting where Holy Scripture is concerned, and which alone is able to pronounce a discourse which can receive God's blessing. Let us then apply ourselves to our text; the true exegete will always find in it fresh depths and new mysteries; like a child in a marvellous garden, he will be filled with wonder. But let him not pose as God's advocate!

Be faithful to the text and faithful to life. It is always better to keep too close to the text than to adhere too closely to one subject or dwell too long on it. Be bold and yet humble; great courage is always needed, and also great humility, but let the accent be on humility so that love of God may be fulfilled in love of one's neighbour.

5. *Composing the Sermon*

There are a number of rules which should be observed in composing a sermon. First, a sermon should be *written*; this is so important that it is necessary to give reasons for it. Certainly the preacher will be giving an address, but whether or not he has the necessary capacity for doing so, he should not simply wait for the Holy Spirit, or any other spirit, to inspire him at the moment of speaking. A sermon must be prepared and drafted word by word. It is certainly true in this instance that an account will have to be given for every idle word. Preaching is not an art in which some are able to improvise while others have to write everything out; it is the central action of evangelical worship, in close association with the sacrament. Only a sermon in which every word can be justified may be said to be a sacramental action. The responsibility which attaches to every word he utters, is a part of the sanctification of the minister. This rule holds for every preacher and not only for the young. Some ministers have acquired such facility in preaching that they feel able to dispense with this discipline, but their sermons are not Christian discourses. A sermon should not be merely a chatty talk, obviously delivered without preparation.

Is an introduction necessary? Not unless it is a biblical introduction; any other kind is to be ruled out for several reasons, two of which may be noted:

1. Why do we go to church? To hear the Word of God: thus the successive acts of worship are sufficient introduction to the sermon—which is their culmination. A few opening words will suffice: any other sort of introduction is waste of time—and a sermon should not be too long. But some sermons are too short, and in their defence it is urged that brevity is a virtue. This may be true for any other sort of discourse, but not for preaching, which must make room for the Word of God and the Word will regulate the length of the sermon; obviously mere length is not a sign of faithfulness; nevertheless it must not be forgotten that the sermon is included in the worship offered to God and that worship is the most important part of Sunday. One does not give glory to God with an eye on the clock.

2. Only too often an introduction diverts the thoughts from the Word of God. People come to church with all kinds of preoccupations in their minds, and then the minister wastes words on what is not the real subject of his discourse. From the outset he misses his mark, for the first ten minutes are of prime importance in indicating what the sermon is to be.

If, however, there must be an introduction, how is it to be done?

(a) A favourite point of departure is to speak about the contemporary situation, towards which the minister may take a favourable or a negative attitude. But the audience probably knows more about this than the speaker, and it has no bearing on the sermon.

(b) Or perhaps one may begin by quoting a great man; but what significance has this man's name in the context of prayer and reading? The only result is to turn the congregation's thinking into another direction. The Word of the Bible cannot gain credit from that of a man, however notable. This is unworthy.

(c) The introduction may be negative, but this procedure is bad. An account of the sins and the errors of the world is not a good way to begin a sermon. It may offer a wide horizon but it is not legitimate to deluge a Christian community, or one on the way to becoming Christian, with such an outburst of bitterness at the very start. Of the same sort is the scheme which begins by abusing the old Adam which persists in man in order to counter it with a resounding 'But God . . .' To begin by describing man's corruption may easily lead to thematic preaching and the Bible will remain in the background.

(d) Sometimes a preacher will make use, by way of opening remarks, of a piece of biblical theology or an introduction to the Old or the New Testament. This is out of place as a separate section of the sermon, but may well fit into the exposition of the text.

An attempt is sometimes made to justify an introductory section on theological grounds. The starting point is the notion that there is in man's nature something that responds to the Word of God and disposes him to hear it. This might indeed have been true of Adam in Paradise! Such a point of view would be conceivable in the structure of Roman theology. But according to the Reformers' understanding of the Bible, there are no such human potentialities; the relationship between man and God is effected from on high by a divine miracle. Man is not naturally disposed to hear the Word of God : we are children of wrath (Eph. 2.3).

We appeal to men on the grounds that they are called to baptism in Christ. They possess nothing except the promise; but, because of the promise, human nature need not be regarded from a purely negative point of view; here is the real significance of John 3.16. We believe in the miracle

wrought by God in us, and by which a relationship between
ourselves and God is brought into being. It is unthinkable
that a man should attempt to speak of this, but nevertheless
this is what he is called to do. But he has only to play the
part of a messenger who has a message to deliver; he must
not try to build a stair up which to climb; he does not have
to ascend the heights, for, in truth, what happens is that
something comes down from on high to us, but only if,
from the start, it is the Bible that speaks.

A sermon is not made up of separate parts arbitrarily
arranged in relation to the text; it is a whole. If it is considered as body or *corpus*, then necessarily any premedi-
tated arrangement is excluded. In a thematic discourse it is
logical to distinguish the several parts, but this is not how
the preacher of the Gospel proceeds. He is guided by the
text, not by a topic. Thus the Law will not be separated
from the Gospel; neither will faith be discussed first from
a theoretical and then from a practical point of view. Unity
arises from the text itself if its own rhythm be followed
and its proportions observed. Thus, it is necessary to proceed verse by verse, though it may be that not all the verses
are of the same quality and that there are variations of
emphasis in the text. However that may be, the essential
content of the text must govern the development. For
example, in John 1.43-52 the discourse will turn on verses
47-48 : Christ recognizes the predestined Nathanael; all the
rest is directed towards this central point.

There is, therefore, no need to consider what has to be
said firstly, secondly, and thirdly, Take note of what is said,
for it is unique : it is the Word of God and it owes nothing
to man's ingenuity; he can only bear witness to it.

A sermon does not require a set conclusion; it comes to
an end when it reaches the end of its text. If a conclusion
is necessary to sum up what has been said, then the
preacher has missed the mark. Neither should the application form the conclusion, for then the challenge will have

been made too late. Quoting parts of the canticles in conclusion, or interpolating them arbitrarily in the body of the
discourse, should be avoided. It is tempting, and dangerous,
to conclude with a great Alleluia in the guise of a final
exhortation. This may happen, but it cannot be an habitual
method.

Finally the last word : *amen* is a consolation to us in our
weakness. Because we believe that the Word of God is
truth, we have tried to bear witness to it. This *amen* gives
us peace and calls us to work, with confidence, on our next
sermon.

APPENDIX

OUTLINE SERMONS

Dr Barth included these three outlines in *La Proclamation de l'Evangile* 'to illustrate what has been said'.

1. *Psalm 121*

This psalm comprises four parts:

(a) *Verses 1-2* represent a pilgrims' hymn and tell of the help God gives to one who is weak and distressed. Such a one knows that there is help for him and, furthermore, he knows whence it comes. He turns his eyes in that direction, that is to say, towards Jerusalem where dwells the Lord God, the Almighty, Maker of heaven and earth. That is the place from which help comes. So for us also there is a place whence we may await deliverance.

(b) *Verses 3-4.* This assurance is ours because God—our help—is active, he works; he never sleeps, he is never in-accessible to the man who has need of him. He is never far away, existing impassively in spheres far removed from contact with this world. On the contrary, the Lord is present and close at hand and we can always find him.

(c) *Verses 5-6.* God protects us precisely when the danger is greatest and threatens to overwhelm us. Here the historical element plays no part. Local extremes of weather, caused by sun or moon, are quite secondary and have no importance for our interpretation.

(d) *Verses 7-8.* The Old Testament community was in the habit of praying for each of its members and found strength and consolation in this mutual intercession. We also, today, know that there is someone who prays for us, but how much more effectively than was then the case! Christ himself intercedes for us with God, the Almighty. His prayer is our hope and our strength.

A sermon on Psalm 121 might follow this scheme; there is no question here of any particular theme.

2. John 13.33-35

These three verses are very suitable for a sermon in Passion-tide. They are, of course, closely linked to what goes before them. Verse 30 marks the last and final phase of the passion of the Son of Man. At that moment, in that night, the incarnation of God is accomplished : one last and supreme glorifying is assured him in his very humiliation (verse 31). At the same time he is glorified in his approaching elevation. The step which Jesus is about to take towards the profoundest depths of suffering already proclaims his transfiguration, his passing into glory.

At verse 33 a new element is introduced. *Little children . . . I say to you . . .* These words are addressed in the first place to the little group of disciples who are present, but this group already embraces the whole believing world : the entire community of believers exists in these few apostles. Jesus communicates to them and to all his last thoughts. They have to learn and understand that they cannot follow Christ along this path; neither the world nor the Church will be able to imitate what has been given to Christ alone to do. He alone is able to tread the road marked out for him by the Father, and he will follow it for the sake of the world.

But at verse 34 there appears, surprisingly, a new commandment. This command does not enjoin imitation : it requires mutual love. Obedience responds to the direct order, *Love one another*, for love has become the new nature of those who have seen Jesus. But the world has to hear the words of Jesus through the mediation of the Church and its members, and this will only be carried out *if you have love for one another*. We are not told that the whole world will be won by these words of Jesus, but that the behaviour of the disciples will show whether they are with Jesus. This behaviour is the characteristic mark of the Church in the world.

This outline is only a suggestion, meant to give some help in discerning the main themes in the text; it is not intended as a model to be copied. The preacher's task is to put into common speech for the man of today what is to be found in the text. But these few verses are a mine of inexhaustible riches.

3. *Ephesians 2.1-10*

This passage raises in an acute form the problem of preaching about sin. At the outset it establishes the fact that those whom the apostle is addressing were men of this world and consequently sunk in sin, living in that condition as rebellious beings, cut off from God. This situation is not life at all; these men were dead in the true meaning of the word, under the wrath of God. At verse 3, in which the concrete and terrible reality of sin is brought into sharp relief, a startling reversal breaks in: 'you' is abruptly followed by 'we' as Paul confesses himself also, like these others, to be lost in sin.

But immediately we are shown an amazing thing, sin in its totality is cast away into the past. This in no way implies any weakening of the consciousness of sin; on the contrary, its hateful character is all the more clearly revealed. The shocking reality and abiding presence of sin remain even though it has been relegated to a time which lies behind us. Sin is there at all times, but it has been repulsed and vanquished; its power to dominate and to destroy has been taken from it.

Verses 4-7 point to the victor who has conquered all that bears the mark of sin. The good news rings out: all you who lay dead under the yoke of sin are raised to life in Christ. This resurrection of the dead is the work of God and of God only, accomplished in Christ and in his lifting up. The fight against sin is far behind, the battle has been won though it is not yet at an end. Victory is assured. In this fashion Paul attacks evil. There is no system of morality, no plan of campaign, no ethical precepts; only a turning to him who once for all has stripped sin of its power. This reference to Christ is developed in verse 7. Christians, as Paul sees them, are the objects of God's goodness; in his immeasurable riches God has prepared for us an incorruptible heritage.

Verses 8-10 relate to the time between the resurrection of Christ and his return. What we are in this intermediate period owes nothing to ourselves. We have, therefore, no reason and no right to glorify ourselves. It is not our own works which make us what we are, but the grace of God which has saved us through faith, which itself is God's gift. Where then shall we find any cause for boasting? And, moreover, we are created for the doing of good works. It is important to note that Paul uses the indicative and avoids the imperative in order to rule out the slightest doubt on this point: all is the work of God, nothing is due to man's initiative.

This passage is typical of the apostolic witness, which is never concerned to discuss a particular theme but submits itself solely to the one great theme of the Bible. This message must be given clearly to the Christian congregation.

A SERMON ON ASCENSION DAY

This sermon, preached in Basel Prison in 1956, is reproduced from *Deliverance to the Captives*. See p. 65 of *Prayer and Preaching*.

O LORD our God! Our father through thy Son who became our brother!

Thou callest us: 'Return, you sons of man! Lift up your hearts! Seek what is above!' With these words thou hast summoned us this very morning. Here we are, each one with his life which is not his own, but wholly thine, wholly in thy hands; each one with his sins, great and small, which only thou canst forgive; each one with his sorrows which only thou canst transform into joy. Here we are nevertheless each one also with his own secret hope that thou wilt prove to be his almighty and merciful God.

We all know that only one thing will please and honour thee—earnest asking for thy Spirit, earnest searching for thy truth, earnest longing for thy help and guidance. We also know that even these can only be thy work in us. Wake us up, O Lord, that we may be awake!

Grant that everything we do in this hour be according to thy will, when we pray and sing, when we speak and listen, when we partake of the Lord's Supper. Grant this request to all that join us today in celebrating the Ascension of our Lord Jesus Christ, even the bedridden in the hospitals, the mentally disturbed of our local institution, the countless crowd of those unaware that they themselves are prisoners, are sick or disturbed, and perhaps have never heard of thee as their comfort, their hope and their redeemer. Shed thy light upon them and upon us, through Jesus Christ, our Lord. Amen.

Look up to him, your face will shine, and you shall never be ashamed.
                                                              PSALM 34.5

My dear brothers and sisters, '*Look up to him!*' This is
what we commemorate on Ascension Day: the urgent invitation, the permission and the command, the freedom we
enjoy as Christians and the obedience that is expected
from us to look up to him, to Jesus Christ, who lived for
us, died and rose again. He is our Saviour who watches
over us like an older brother watches over his younger
brothers and sisters, yet in his protection is also their
example and their master.

He is above, in *heaven*. We are below, on earth. When
we hear the word 'heaven' we are inclined to think of the
great blue or grey sphere arching over us with its sun-
shine, its clouds and its rain, or of the even higher world of
the stars. This is what we may have in mind right now. In
the vocabulary of the Bible, however, this 'heaven' is nothing but the sign of an even higher reality. There is a realm
above and beyond the world of man, which is lost to our
sight, to our understanding, to our penetration, and even
more to our dominion. It is way above and beyond us. In
biblical language heaven is the dwelling place, the throne,
of God. It is the mystery encompassing us everywhere.
There Jesus Christ lives. He is in the centre of this mystery
beyond. Of all men, he alone went there, all by himself, in
order to be there and from there, from the throne of God,
the Lord and Saviour of us all. Therefore: *Look up to him!*

To 'look up' alone would not do. 'Chin up!' we are wont
to say to a friend in distress. You may have heard this
'chin up!' yourself. But this is somewhat of a problem.
Could it not be that above and beyond us, in heaven, we
are confronted with a stark and merciless mirror, reflecting
our own human affliction? We might see once more the
wrong done to us by our neighbours and the wrong done
by us to them, but now magnified and projected into the
infinite. We might see our guilt, our inner anxieties and

our outward affliction, all we call fate, and finally death itself. All these could be included in the mystery beyond, in heaven! This heaven would lie like a dark cloud over our heads, or like one of those dungeons where they used to keep prisoners in centuries gone-by, or even like a coffin lid, burying us alive under its weight. Does anyone wish to look up there? No, we'd better forget about such a menace from above! But what is the use of trying not to think of it if it is nevertheless real? Things could even be much worse. God himself could be like this heaven: a Holy Being, right-fully turned against us, a sinister tyrant, the very enemy of mankind, or perhaps simply an indifferent God who willed for unknown reasons to set us under this cloud, under this dungeon, under this coffin lid. Many of us, even all of us in our desperate moments and years, hold on to this mental picture of heaven and of God. No, 'look up' by itself would be no help at all.

But to look up to him, to Jesus Christ—this is our help! He is over us. He is in the centre of that encompassing mystery. He is in heaven. Who is Jesus Christ? He is the man in whom God has not only expressed his love, not only painted it on the wall, but put it to work. He is the principal actor who has taken upon himself and has over-come our human affliction, the injustice done by ourselves and by everybody else, our guilt and anxiety, our fate, even our death. These evils no longer threaten us from above. They are below us, even under our feet. He is the Son of God, who was made man in our likeness, who became our brother, in order that we may be with him children of the Father, that we may all be reunited with God and may share in his blessings: in his severe kindness and in his kind severity, and lastly in the eternal life for which we are meant and which is meant for us. This Jesus Christ, this mighty man, this Son of God is in heaven. And so is God. In the face of the Son the face of the heavenly Father is made to shine.

'Look up *to him*!' This means: Let him be who he is, above us, in heaven. Acknowledge and believe that he is up there and lives for us! Keep firmly in mind that he intervenes with all his power in your behalf, but keep firmly in mind also that you belong to him and not to yourselves. Say very simply 'yes'. Say that he is right and wants to make things right for you, indeed has already made them right for us all. Is this an exaggerated claim? Has he really made things right for all of us? Even for the most miserable, the most afflicted and the most embittered of human beings? Yes! Even for the most grievous offenders? Yes! Even for the godless—or those pretending to be godless, as may be the case with some of your fellow-prisoners who declined to be with us this morning? Yes! Jesus Christ has made things right for them and for us all. He is willing to do it time and again. To look up to Jesus Christ means to accept his righteousness and to be content; not to question any more that he is right. This is the message of the Ascension: we are invited to look up to him, to this Jesus Christ, or, to use a more familiar expression, to believe in him.

'Look up to him *and your face will shine*!' What an announcement! What a promise and assurance! People, very ordinary human beings, with illumined faces! Not angels in heaven, but men and women on earth! Not some lucky inhabitants of a beautiful island far away, but people here in Basel, here in this house! Not some very special people among us, but each and every one of us! Might this be the true meaning of the promise? Yes, this is the true meaning. But is this the only real meaning? Yes, this is the only real meaning. Look up to him, and your face will shine!

When a man, any one of us, obeys this imperative and looks up to him, to Jesus Christ, a momentous change takes place in him. The greatest revolution is unimportant by comparison. The transformation cannot be overlooked. It is manifest, quite simply, in so much as he who looks up to him and believes in him, here on earth, here in Basel, here in this house, may become a child of God. It is an inward change, yet it cannot possibly remain hidden. As soon as it occurs, it presses forcefully for outward manifestation. A great and enduring light brightly dawns on such a person. This light is reflected on his face, in his eyes, in his behaviour, in his words and deeds. Such a person experiences joy in the midst of his sorrows and sufferings, much as he still may sigh and grumble. Not a cheap and superficial joy that passes, but deep-seated, lasting joy. It transforms man in his sadness into a fundamentally joyful being. We may as well admit it: he has got something to laugh at, and he just cannot help laughing, even though he does not feel like it. His laughter is not bad, but good, not a mockery, but an open and relaxing laughter, not a diplomatic gesture as has recently become so fashionable in politics, but honest and sincere laughter, coming from the bottom of man's heart. Such light and joy and laughter are ours when we look up to him, to Jesus Christ. He is the one who makes us radiant. We ourselves cannot put on bright faces. But neither can we prevent them from shining. Looking up to him, our faces shine.

Dear brothers and sisters, why is it then that our faces are not bright? If they were, we would feel fine, would be glad to live uprightly and contentedly in spite of adversities, wouldn't we? Just because we would feel fine, we would be radiant. But something more important has to be considered here. If the light, the joy and the laughter of God's children really pressed for outward manifestation and became visible, our fellowmen around us would notice it in the first place. Don't you agree with me that such a change would make a quite definite impact on them? It would be a sign that there are different and far better things in store than they are wont to see. It would give them confidence, courage and hope. They would be re-

lieved, as we have been relieved this last week by the sun
after a long winter. Why relieved? Because such a bright
face would be the reflection of heaven on earth, of Jesus
Christ, of God the Father himself. What a relief that light
would be for them and for us! Do we not all together long
for its appearance?

We should get the simple truth straight, dear friends. We
are in the world not to comfort ourselves, but to comfort
others. Yet the one and only genuine comfort we may offer
to our fellowmen is this reflection of heaven, of Jesus
Christ, of God himself, as it appears on a radiant face. Why
don't we do it? Why do we withhold from them the one
comfort of mutual benefit? Why are the faces we show
each other at best superior looking, serious, questioning,
sorrowful and reproachful faces, at worst even grimaces or
lifeless masks, real Carnival masks? Why don't our faces
shine?

Let me say only one thing here. It could easily be otherwise. We could greet each other with bright faces! We
could comfort each other. We, here, today! Where the
Spirit of the Lord is, there is freedom for man to comfort
his neighbour. 'He who believes in me,' says Jesus Christ
himself in another Scripture passage, 'out of his heart shall
flow rivers of living water.' This happens when we look up
to him. No one has ever looked up to him without this
miracle happening. No one who gets slowly used to looking
up to him has failed to glimpse light around him. The dark
earth on which we live has always become bright whenever
man looked up to him, and believed in him.

'Look up to him, your face will shine, *and you shall
never be ashamed.*' I just mentioned the 'dark' earth. Reading the newspapers, looking around at the world and into
our own hearts and lives, we can't possibly deny that the
earth is really dark, that we live in a world to be afraid in.
Why afraid? Because we all live under the threat of being
put to shame, and rightly so. This would not only imply

that we have blundered here and there, but that our whole life, with all our thoughts, desires and accomplishments, might be in truth, in God's judgment and verdict, a failure, an infamy, a total loss. This is the great threat. This is why the ground shakes under our feet, the sky is covered with clouds, and the earth, so beautifully created, darkens. Indeed we should be put to shame.

But now we hear the very opposite. 'You shall never be ashamed.' What I would like to do, dear brothers and sisters, is to ask you, each and all, to get up together and like a choir repeat: 'We must never be ashamed!' Each one would have to repeat it for himself and lastly I would repeat it for myself: 'I must never be ashamed!' This is what counts. We shall not be, I shall not be ashamed, not when looking up to him. Not because we deserve to be spared the shame! Not even because our faces shine when raised to him. Our radiance will be and must be a sign that we will not be put to shame. It is an evidence of the relationship established between God and ourselves. And this is the power of the relationship: what is true and valid in heaven, what Jesus Christ has done for us, what has been accomplished by him, man's redemption, justification and preservation, is true and valid on earth also. The Father does not put us, his children, to shame when we look up to Jesus. In consequence we, his children, may never be ashamed. This we may know, this may be our strength, this may be our life, if only we look up to him, fearlessly and brightly. May each one repeat in his heart: 'Bless the Lord, O my soul; and all that is within me, bless his holy name! Bless the Lord, O my soul, and forget not all his benefits; who forgives all your iniquity, who heals all your diseases, who redeems your life from the pit, who crowns you with steadfast love and mercy.' With these words let us go to the Lord's Supper. Amen.

O Lord, our God! We are grateful that all is as we have

tried to say with our weak words and to hear with our
weak ears. Our praise of thy name will never cease, because thy mercy and truth are without end, and are always
greater and more glorious than we may ever express or
grasp.

Bring about the first fruits of thy spirit in our hearts and
lives, and in all we shall think and say and do today and
tomorrow! Grant us to be faithful stewards of thy gifts,
making good use of the time which thou hast given to work
for its fulfilment, for thy glory and our salvation!

Continue to have mercy on us and on all men, on our
families, on all the suffering and tempted, on the authorities of this town and country, on civil servants, teachers
and students, on the judges, the accused and the sentenced,
on the pastors and their congregations, on the missionaries
and those to whom they are privileged to proclaim thy
truth, on the Evangelicals in Spain and in South America
and on their misguided oppressors. Where thou dost not
build through thy word, Church and world are built in
vain. Let thy word run its course and reach many. Let it go
to all men with the power to shine, to heal and to win
which it has whenever it is rightly preached and received
in the power of thy Holy Spirit.

'Our Father . . .'